SCOTTISH WONDER TALES
FROM MYTH AND LEGEND

THE COMING OF BRIDE

From the painting by John Duncan, A.R.S.A.

Illustrations

Introduction

The myths and legends of Scotland are full of what is called "local colour". They afford us not only glimpses of ancient times and of old habits of thought and life, but also of the country itself at different times of the year. In the winter season the great mountain ranges are white with snow and many inland lochs are frozen over, but along the west coast, which is washed by the warm surface waters of the Atlantic and bathed in mild moist breezes from the south-west, there may be found sheltered and sunny spots where wild flowers continue to bloom. The old people believed that somewhere in the west the spirit of Spring had its hiding-place, and they imagined this hiding-place to be a green floating island on which the sun always shone and flowers were always blooming. During the reign of Beira[1], Queen of Winter, the spirit of Spring, they thought, was always trying to visit Scotland, and they imagined that Beira raised the storms of January and February to prolong her reign by keeping the grass from growing. Beira was regarded as a hard and cruel old woman, and the story of her exploits is the story of the weather conditions in winter and early spring. She rouses the dangerous whirlpool of Corryvreckan, she brings the snow, she unlooses the torrents that cause rivers to overflow. According to folk belief, it was she who formed the lochs and the mountains. In the days when the people had no calendar, the various periods of good and bad weather were named after the battles of Beira and the victories of the spirits of sunshine and growth. Gaelic-speaking people still refer to certain gales in February and March by their ancient names— the "whistling wind", the "sweeper", and so on, as set forth in the second chapter. On the northeast coast even those fisher folks, who are not Gaelic speakers, still tell that the fierce southwesterly gales of early spring are caused by the storm-wife whom they call "Gentle Annie". This Annie may be the same old deity as Black Annis of Leicestershire and Anu of Ireland, whose name lingers in the place name, the "Paps of Anu", a

[1] Pronounced Bee'ra.

mountain group in County Kerry. In Scotland the story of the winter goddess, Beira, has a strictly local setting. She is, in consequence, a local deity. Bride, the lady of summer growth, is still remembered also, and there are beautiful Gaelic songs about her.

Other stories have likewise a local character. Those who know the west coast will be familiar with the glorious transparency of the hill-surrounded lochs in calm weather. When the old people saw the waters reflecting the mountains and forests, the bare cliffs and the bright girths of green verdure, they imagined a " Land-under-Waves " about which they, of course, made stories. The "Northern Lights" (aurora borealis), which are a feature of northern winters, also stirred their imaginations. They called these vivid and beautiful streamers " Nimble Men " and " Merry Dancers ", and believed they sometimes danced and sometimes waged war. In the red-spotted green stones called "blood stones" they saw the blood-drops of the wounded. When the streamers are particularly bright a red cloud often appears below them; this the old people called " the pool of fairy blood ".

In like manner they accounted for the restlessness of the waters of a strait between the island of Lewis and the Shant islands by imagining that Blue Men were always swimming up and down this haunt of theirs, trying to sink boats and ships. As the Gaelic people have ever been great lovers of poetry, they made the Blue Men poets, and told that they spared those seafarers who were able to complete the half verses they shouted to them, by way of challenge, for trial of skill. The "Blue Men" are peculiar to Scotland, and especially to the north-western area.

In other stories we find female water spirits who wait at fords, threatening travellers with disaster. They also could be thwarted by those who had the necessary knowledge which made it possible for them to secure protection.

Almost all the rivers of Scotland were abodes of goddesses, but about many of them there are no surviving stories. The character of a goddess was suggested by that of a river. The goddess of the river Forth, for instance, was "the deaf or soundless one", because the Forth is a comparatively silent river; the goddess of the Clyde, on the other hand, was "the purifying one", because the old people knew it as a river which scoured the country it passed through, and carried much mud and clay seaward when in flood.[1]

Many old stories have been lost, of course, and those which remain are mere fragments of an ancient mythology. In different parts of Scot-

[1] Professor W. J. Watson's Rhind lectures, 1916.

land there are variations of legends, because the local conditions are of varying character.

Readers may ask how the stories of ancient beliefs happen to be preserved in Christian times. One reason is because they are connected with place names; another because certain of them were recorded centuries ago by early writers. One of the early Scottish collectors of old legends and poems was Sir James MacGregor, Dean of Lismore, who lived in the sixteenth century. His manuscript volume is still in existence, and the most of it can be read without difficulty. It is called "The Dean of Lismore's Book".

The greater number of collected legends, however, have been taken down from reciters in recent times. In the days when there were no books, poets and story-tellers committed their compositions to memory. These they repeated to their students, who in turn repeated them to others. In this way poems and stories were handed down from generation to generation. Even in our own day it is possible to find not a few Gaelic-speaking men and women who can repeat compositions many thousands of words in length which they have learned by rote. The writer knew an old woman whose stories would have filled a volume quite as large as this one. Some of the poems collected by the Dean of Lismore in the sixteenth century were still repeated about a generation ago, almost word for word, by old reciters in the Highlands, certain of whom could neither read nor write.

Men and women able to repeat popular poems and stories have always been greatly thought of in the Gaelic-speaking parts of Scotland. On long, dark winter nights it is still the custom in small villages for friends to collect in a house and hold what they call a "ceilidh" (pronounced kay'lee). Young and old are entertained by the reciters of old poems and legendary stories which deal with ancient beliefs, the doings of traditional heroes and heroines, and so on. Some sing old and new songs set to old music or new music composed in the manner of the old. In this way some of the ancient poems, stories, and music of the early inhabitants of Scotland have been preserved till our own times.

The wonder tales of Scotland do not afford a very clear indication of the attitude of worshippers towards their deities. So far as can be gathered, they loved and admired some deities, especially those that brought them good luck and plenty, and they hated and feared those deities who were supposed to cause suffering and disaster. At the same time they believed that there were mysterious Powers, or a Power, greater than the gods and goddesses.

Beira, the winter queen, might raise storms and

bring snow and frost, but when the spring season came on she could not prevent the grass growing or the trees budding. The Powers which caused the seasons to change were never named; they were not even given human attributes. When we study the customs and search through the stories ·for traces of religious beliefs and practices, we find that there were many ceremonies, some of which still survive. The old people appear to have been greatly concerned about the earth, the water supply, and the weather. When they took oaths they swore by the earth. In one old story, for instance, a hero is insulted and badly treated by his enemies. He complains to his companions. "When", this story runs, "he rehearsed to them the tale of his wanderings, and told of the insults and of the bad treatment he had received, and the hardships he had endured since they had separated, *they lifted a little piece of earth and they shouted 'Vengeance'*." That is, they swore by what was holiest to them. In various parts of Scotland there are earth mounds which used to be sacred to the old people. They held regular assemblies upon them, at which new laws were made and law-breakers were judged. Religious ceremonies were also performed. When Christianity was introduced, the sacred mounds and the lands surrounding them were, in many cases, taken over as church-lands. The Gaelic name for "church-lands" is derived from the name of an earth goddess, and rendered in English as "Navity" or "Navie". No doubt Beira, who was a goddess of the mountains, lochs, and rivers, as well as of the weather, had some connection with the earth spirit. She kept herds of wild animals, like the Greek Artemis. At the same time she found the "Powers", which caused the grass to grow, were opposed to her when spring came on. The period of her reign was limited to winter, and during winter the "Powers" favoured her.

The earth Power, or Powers, may also have had control over the fairies who were usually clad in green, which was a supernatural colour. It is still regarded unlucky for ladies to wear green dresses. An old Scottish saying is:

> A Graham in green
> Should never be seen.

In Wales one of the names of the fairies is Y Mamau, which means "The Mothers". It may be the fairies represent the ancient group of "Earth Mothers" who caused the grass to grow, the corn seeds to sprout in the earth, the trees to bud, blossom, and bear fruit. The fairies are always represented as busy workers; they teach human beings how to compose music and make musical instruments, how to make implements

and weapons, and so on; and they sometimes
assist them to spin and weave, to sow seeds, to
plough and to reap. The people made food offerings to the fairies, who were very fond of meal.
Mothers used to put meal in children's pockets
to protect them against the fairies.

Certain animals were connected with the earth
spirit or spirits. One was the boar, and there are
references in Gaelic stories to a "green boar"
and a fierce "black boar". In the northern
and southern Highlands there long existed a
prejudice against pork, because pigs were, it
seems, sacred animals. The devil is sometimes
called the "Black Pig", because the early Chris-
tians regarded the Pagan gods as demons. Another sacred animal was the serpent. All winter
long it slept secure from storms and cold. When,
however, Beira, the winter goddess, was over-
thrown, and Bride, the goddess of growth, began
her reign, the serpent came forth from its winter
abode. The people then chanted a hymn, of
which the following is a verse:—

> To-day is the Day of Bride,
> The serpent shall come from his hole,
> I will not molest the serpent,
> And the serpent will not molest me.

The serpent was sometimes called "Daughter
of Ivor", and MacIvors were supposed to be safe
from attack by her and all other serpents. She

was also referred to as "noble queen". It is possible she was a form of the Earth spirit in spring-time. Another verse of a Bride's Day hymn is:—

> The serpent will come from the hole
> On the brown day of Bride,
> Though there should be three feet of snow
> On the flat surface of the ground.[1]

A white serpent was supposed to give skill to physicians. A part of the body was cooked, and he who first tasted the juice of the serpent obtained power to cure diseases. This belief will be found in the story about Michael Scott.

The salmon was a sacred fish, and he who likewise first tasted the juice of a certain salmon obtained the power to foretell events. When the first salmon grilse of the season is caught, salmon fishers on the east coast make merry and celebrate the event, as probably did their pagan ancestors in ancient times. On several of the old standing stones of Scotland there are drawings of salmon. Serpents are also depicted.

How did the old people worship the earth and other spirits? The answer is that they made offerings to them, and performed ceremonies to secure luck and protect themselves against attack. Instead of prayers they used magical verses. Various charms were repeated to cure diseases and ward

[1] Dr. A. Carmichael's *Carmina Gadelica*, Vol. I, p. 169.

off trouble. Here is an extract from a charm
against the "evil eye":—

> The eye that went over,
> And came back,
> That reached the bone,
> And reached the marrow,
> I will lift from off thee—
> And the King of the Elements will aid me.

The person who repeated the charm believed
that the injurious influence of the "evil eye"
would be "lifted off" with the aid of the "King
of the Elements". We do not have any stories
about this god. He is often referred to, and is
one of the vague Powers without a personal name.

On "Bride's Day", the first day of the Gaelic
Spring, offerings were made to earth and sea.
Milk was poured on the ground, and the fisher
people made porridge and threw it into the sea
so that the sea might yield what was sought from
it—lots of fish, and also seaweed for fertilizing
the soil. In some parts of the Hebrides the sea
deity to whom the food offerings were made was
called "Shony".

It will thus be seen that the old stories are not
only interesting as stories, but are worthy of
study as helping us to know something about the
beliefs of the people of olden time.

Certain stories appear to be very ancient. It
is possible that one or two have come down from

the Late Stone Age, which, in these islands, closed probably about 3000 years ago. There are hints of very ancient beliefs, for instance, in the story about "Finlay and the Giants". The hero obtains a magic wand which transforms stone pillars into human beings. It was believed by the old people that the spirit of the dead entered the stone erected over a grave. Another story of special interest is the one about "Heroes on the Green Isle". A princess is confined in a tower, waiting for a hero to win her as his bride by taking her down. A similar story is found in an ancient Egyptian papyrus. It may be that the Scottish and Egyptian versions of this legend came from the same source in remote times. A string of Egyptian beads has been found in a grave near Stonehenge. It came from Egypt about 3000 years ago, along the old trade routes. If far-travelled wanderers, or traders, brought beads, they may also have brought some stories. The ancient Egyptians had, like the ancient folk of Scotland, a wonder tale about a floating island which vanished beneath the waves.

Another interesting Scottish story is "The Vision of the Dead". The woman who acts as a nurse to a fairy child sees the spirits of the dead cutting corn. In Egypt it was believed that the dead were thus employed in the Paradise of Osiris, who was, among other things, a corn god.

The gods and goddesses of Scotland were never depicted by sculptors like the gods and goddesses of ancient Greece. They are not therefore so well known. They would have been entirely forgotten long ago had not the old bards sung songs about them, and the old story-tellers composed "wonder tales", such as are retold in this volume from fragments that survive.

Of special interest at the present time are the references in some stories to "red moss"; that is, the red "sphagnum" which was used to dress wounds. Apparently the ancient people knew from experience that it had cleansing and healing properties, and esteemed the red as superior to green sphagnum. They also used tar water for skin troubles, and to cure diseases they used certain herbs from which some modern-day medicines are manufactured.

CHAPTER I

Beira, Queen of Winter

Dark Beira was the mother of all the gods and goddesses in Scotland. She was of great height and very old, and everyone feared her. When roused to anger she was as fierce as the biting north wind and harsh as the tempest-stricken sea. Each winter she reigned as Queen of the Four Red Divisions of the world, and none disputed her sway. But when the sweet spring season drew nigh, her subjects began to rebel against her and to long for the coming of the Summer King, Angus of the White Steed, and Bride, his beautiful queen, who were loved by all, for they were the bringers of plenty and of bright and happy days. It enraged Beira greatly to find her power passing away, and she tried her utmost to prolong the winter season by raising spring storms and sending blighting frost to kill early flowers and keep the grass from growing.

Beira lived for hundreds and hundreds of years. The reason she did not die of old age was because, at the beginning of every spring, she drank the magic waters of the Well of Youth which bubbles up in the Green Island of the West. This was a floating island where summer was the only season, and the trees were always bright with blossom and laden with fruit. It drifted about on the silver tides of the blue Atlantic, and sometimes appeared off the western coasts of Ireland and sometimes close to the Hebrides. Many bold mariners have steered their galleys up and down the ocean, searching for Green Island in vain. On a calm morning they might sail past its shores and yet never know it was near at hand, for oft-times it lay hidden in a twinkling mist. Men have caught glimpses of it from the shore, but while they gazed on its beauties with eyes of wonder, it vanished suddenly from sight by sinking beneath the waves like the setting sun. Beira, however, always knew where to find Green Island when the time came for her to visit it.

The waters of the Well of Youth are most potent when the days begin to grow longer, and most potent of all on the first of the lengthening days of spring. Beira always visited the island on the night before the first lengthening day— that is, on the last night of her reign as Queen of Winter. All alone in the darkness she sat beside the Well of Youth, waiting for the dawn. When the first faint beam of light appeared in the eastern sky, she drank the water as it bubbled fresh from a crevice in the rock. It was necessary that she should drink of this magic water before any bird visited the well and before any dog barked. If a bird drank first, or a dog barked ere she began to drink, dark old Beira would crumble into dust.

As soon as Beira tasted the magic water, in silence and alone, she began to grow young again. She left the island and, returning to Scotland, fell into a magic sleep. When, at length, she awoke, in bright sunshine, she rose up as a beautiful girl with long hair yellow as buds of broom, cheeks red as rowan berries, and blue eyes that sparkled like the summer sea in sunshine. Then she went to and fro through Scotland, clad in a robe of green and crowned with a chaplet of bright flowers of many hues. No fairer goddess was to be found in all the land, save Bride, the peerless Queen of Summer.

As each month went past, however, Beira aged quickly. She reached full womanhood in midsummer, and when autumn came on her brows wrinkled and her beauty began to fade. When the season of winter returned once again, she became an old and withered hag, and began to reign as the fierce Queen Beira.

Often on stormy nights in early winter she wandered about, singing this sorrowful song:—

BEIRA

From a drawing by John Duncan, A.R.S.A.

O life that ebbs like the sea!
   I am weary and old, I am weary and old—
Oh! how can I happy be
   All alone in the dark and the cold.

I'm the old Beira again,
   My mantle no longer is green,
I think of my beauty with pain
   And the days when another was queen.

My arms are withered and thin,
   My hair once golden is grey;
'T is winter—my reign doth begin—
   Youth's summer has faded away.

Youth's summer and autumn have fled—
   I am weary and old, I am weary and old.
Every flower must fade and fall dead
   When the winds blow cold, when the winds blow cold.

The aged Beira was fearsome to look upon.
She had only one eye, but the sight of it was keen
and sharp as ice and as swift as the mackerel of
the ocean.　Her complexion was a dull, dark blue,
and this is how she sang about it:—

   Why is my face so dark, so dark?
     So dark, oho! so dark, ohee!
   Out in all weathers I wander alone
     In the mire, in the cold, ah me!

Her teeth were red as rust, and her locks, which
lay heavily on her shoulders, were white as an
aspen covered with hoar frost.　On her head she
wore a spotted mutch.[1]　All her clothing was grey,

---

[1] The old Scottish name for a woman's cap.

and she was never seen without her great dun-coloured shawl, which was drawn closely round her shoulders.

It is told that in the days when the world was young Beira saw land where there is now water and water where there is now land.

Once a wizard spoke to her and said: "Tell me your age, O sharp old woman."

Beira answered: "I have long ceased to count the years. But I shall tell you what I have seen. Yonder is the seal-haunted rock of Skerryvore in the midst of the sea. I remember when it was a mountain surrounded by fields. I saw the fields ploughed, and the barley that grew upon them was sharp and juicy. Yonder is a loch. I remember when it was a small round well. In these days I was a fair young girl, and now I am very old and frail and dark and miserable."

It is told also that Beira let loose many rivers and formed many lochs, sometimes willingly and sometimes against her will, and that she also shaped many bens and glens. All the hills in Ross-shire are said to have been made by Beira.

There was once a well on Ben Cruachan, in Argyll, from which Beira drew water daily. Each morning at sunrise she lifted off the slab that covered it, and each evening at sunset she laid it above the well again. It happened that one evening she forgot to cover the well. Then the proper order of things was disturbed. As soon as the sun went down the water rose in great volume and streamed down the mountain side, roaring like a tempest-swollen sea. When day dawned, Beira found that the valley beneath was filled with water. It was in this way that Loch Awe came to be.

Beira had another well in Inverness-shire which had to be kept covered in like manner from sunset till sunrise. One of her maids, whose name was Nessa, had charge of the well. It happened that one evening the maid was late in going to the well to cover it. When she drew near she beheld the water flowing so fast from it that she turned away and ran for her life. Beira watched her from the top of Ben Nevis, which was her mountain throne, and cried: "You have neglected your duty. Now you will run for ever and never leave water."

The maiden was at once changed into a river, and the loch and the river which runs from it towards the sea were named after her. That is why the loch is called Loch Ness and the river the river Ness.

Once a year, when the night on which she was transformed comes round, Ness (Nessa) arises out of the river in her girl form, and sings a sad sweet song in the pale moonlight. It is said that her voice is clearer and more beautiful than that of any bird, and her music more melodious than the golden harps and silvern pipes of fairyland.

In the days when rivers broke loose and lochs were made, Beira set herself to build the mountains of Scotland. When at work she carried on her back a great creel filled with rocks and earth. Sometimes as she leapt from hill to hill her creel tilted sideways, and rocks and earth fell from it into lochs and formed islands. Many islands are spoken of as "spillings from the creel of the big old woman".

Beira had eight hags who were her servants. They also carried creels, and one after the other they emptied out their creels until a mountain was piled up nigh to the clouds.

One of the reasons why Beira made the mountains was to use them as stepping stones; another was to provide houses for her giant sons. Many of her sons were very quarrelsome; they fought continually one against another. To punish those of them who disobeyed her, Beira shut the offenders up in mountain houses, and from these they could not escape without her permission. But this did not keep them from fighting. Every morning they climbed to the tops of their mountain houses and threw great boulders at one another. That is why so many big grey boulders now lie on steep slopes and are scattered through the valleys. Other giant sons of Beira dwelt in deep caves. Some were horned like deer, and others had many heads. So strong were they that they could pick up cattle and, throwing them over their shoulders, carry them away to roast them for their meals. Each giant son of Beira was called a Fooar.[1]

It was Beira who built Ben Wyvis. She found it a hard task, for she had to do all the work alone, her hag servants being busy elsewhere. One day, when she had grown very weary, she stumbled and upset her creel. All the rocks and earth it contained fell out in a heap, and formed the mountain which is called Little Wyvis.

The only tool that Beira used was a magic hammer. When she struck it lightly on the ground the soil became as hard as iron; when she struck it heavily on the ground a valley was formed. After she had built up a mountain, she gave it its special form by splintering the rocks with her hammer. If she had made all the hills of the same shape, she would not have been able to recognize one from another.

After the mountains were all formed, Beira took great delight in wandering between them and over them. She was always followed by wild animals. The foxes barked with delight when they beheld her, wolves howled to greet her, and

---

[1] Pronounced Foo'ar. The Anglo-Irish rendering is "Fomorian", but the Irish Fomorians are different from the Scottish.

eagles shrieked with joy in mid-air. Beira had great herds and flocks to which she gave her protection—nimble-footed deer, high-horned cattle, shaggy grey goats, black swine, and sheep that had snow-white fleeces. She charmed her deer against the huntsmen, and when she visited a deer forest she helped them to escape from the hunters. During early winter she milked the hinds on the tops of mountains, but when the winds rose so high that the froth was blown from the milking pails, she drove the hinds down to the valleys. The froth was frozen on the crests of high hills, and lay there snow-white and beautiful. When the winter torrents began to pour down the mountain sides, leaping from ledge to ledge, the people said: "Beira is milking her shaggy goats, and streams of milk are pouring down over high rocks."

Beira washed her great shawl in the sea, for there was no lake big enough for the purpose. The part she chose for her washing is the strait between the western islands of Jura and Scarba. Beira's "washing-pot" is the whirlpool, there called Corry-vreckan. It was so named because the son of a Scottish king, named Breckan, was drowned in it, his boat having been upset by the waves raised by Beira.

Three days before the Queen of Winter began her work her hag servants made ready the water for her, and the Corry could then be heard snorting and fuming for twenty miles around. On the fourth day Beira threw her shawl into the whirlpool, and tramped it with her feet until the edge of the Corry overflowed with foam. When she had finished her washing she laid her shawl on the mountains to dry, and as soon as she lifted it up, all the mountains of Scotland were white with snow to signify that the great Queen had begun her reign.

Now, the meaning of this story is that Beira is the spirit of winter. She grows older and fiercer as the weeks go past, until at length her strength is spent. Then she renews her youth, so that she may live through the summer and autumn and begin to reign once again. The ancient people of Scotland saw that during early winter torrents poured down from the hills, and in this Beira fable they expressed their belief that the torrents were let loose by the Winter Queen, and that the lochs were, at the beginning, formed by the torrents that sprang from magic wells. They saw great boulders lying on hillsides and in valleys, and accounted for their presence in these places by telling how they were flung from mountain tops by the giant sons of Beira.

In the next chapter the story will be told of the coming of Angus and Bride, the King and Queen of Summer and Plenty, and of the stormy conflicts waged during the closing weeks of winter and the early weeks of spring between Beira and Angus-the-Ever-Young, who comes from the fabled Green Isle of the West—the land of eternal summer and perpetual youth.

CHAPTER II

The Coming of Angus and Bride

All the long winter Beira kept captive a beautiful young princess named Bride. She was jealous of Bride's beauty, and gave her ragged clothing to wear, and put her to work among the servants in the kitchen of her mountain castle, where the girl had to perform the meanest tasks. Beira scolded her continually, finding fault with everything she did, and Bride's life was made very wretched.

One day Beira gave the princess a brown fleece and said: "You must wash this fleece in the running stream until it is pure white."

Bride took the fleece and went outside the castle, and began to wash it in a pool below a waterfall. All day long she laboured at the work, but to no purpose. She found it impossible to wash the brown colour out of the wool.

When evening came on, Beira scolded the girl, and said: "You are a useless hussy. The fleece is as brown as when I gave it to you."

Said Bride: "All day long have I washed

it in the pool below the waterfall of the Red Rock."

"To-morrow you shall wash it again," Beira said; "and if you do not wash it white, you will go on washing on the next day, and on every day after that.   Now, begone! and do as I bid you."

It was a sorrowful time for Bride.   Day after day she washed the fleece, and it seemed to her that if she went on washing until the world came to an end, the brown wool would never become white.

One morning as she went on with her washing a grey-bearded old man came near.   He took pity on the princess, who wept bitter tears over her work, and spoke to her, saying: "Who are you, and why do you sorrow?"

Said the princess: "My name is Bride.   I am the captive of Queen Beira, and she has ordered me to wash this brown fleece until it is white. Alas! it cannot be done."

"I am sorry for you," the old man said.

"Who are you, and whence come you?" asked Bride.

"My name is Father Winter," the old man told her.   "Give me the fleece, and I shall make it white for you."

Bride gave Father Winter the brown fleece, and when he had shaken it three times it turned white as snow.

The heart of Bride was immediately filled with joy, and she exclaimed: "Dear Father Winter, you are very kind. You have saved me much labour and taken away my sorrow."

Father Winter handed back the fleece to Princess Bride with one hand, and she took it. Then he said: "Take also what I hold in my other hand." As he spoke he gave her a bunch of pure white snowdrops. The eyes of Bride sparkled with joy to behold them.

Said Father Winter: "If Beira scolds you, give her these flowers, and if she asks where you found them, tell her that they came from the green rustling fir-woods. Tell her also that the cress is springing up on the banks of streams, and that the new grass has begun to shoot up in the fields."

Having spoken thus, Father Winter bade the princess farewell and turned away.

Bride returned to the mountain castle and laid the white fleece at Beira's feet. But the old queen scarcely looked at it. Her gaze was fixed on the snowdrops that Bride carried.

"Where did you find these flowers?" Beira asked with sudden anger.

Said Bride: "The snowdrops are now growing in the green rustling fir-woods, the cress is springing up on the banks of streams, and the new grass is beginning to shoot up in the fields."

"Evil are the tidings you bring me!" Beira cried. "Begone from my sight!"

Bride turned away, but not in sorrow. A new joy had entered her heart, for she knew that the wild winter season was going past, and that the reign of Queen Beira would soon come to an end.

Meanwhile Beira summoned her eight hag servants, and spoke to them, saying: "Ride to the north and ride to the south, ride to the east and ride to the west, and I will ride forth also. Smite the world with frost and tempest, so that no flower may bloom and no grass blade survive. I am waging war against all growth."

When she had spoken thus, the eight hags mounted on the backs of shaggy goats and rode forth to do her bidding. Beira went forth also, grasping in her right hand her black magic hammer. On the night of that very day a great tempest lashed the ocean to fury and brought terror to every corner of the land.

Now the reason why Beira kept Bride a prisoner was because her fairest and dearest son, whose name was Angus-the-Ever-Young, had fallen in love with her. He was called "the Ever Young" because age never came near him, and all winter long he lived on the Green Isle of the West, which is also called the "Land of Youth".

Angus first beheld Bride in a dream, and when he awoke he spoke to the King of the Green Isle, saying: "Last night I dreamed a dream and saw a beautiful princess whom I love. Tears fell from her eyes, and I spoke to an old man who stood near her, and said: 'Why does the maiden weep?' Said the old man: 'She weeps because she is kept captive by Beira, who treats her with great cruelty.' I looked again at the princess and said: 'Fain would I set her free.' Then I awoke. Tell me, O king, who is this princess, and where shall I find her?"

The King of the Green Isle answered Angus, saying: "The fair princess whom you saw is Bride, and in the days when you will be King of Summer she will be your queen. Of this your mother, Queen Beira, has full knowledge, and it is her wish to keep you away from Bride, so that her own reign may be prolonged. Tarry here, O Angus, until the flowers begin to bloom and the grass begins to grow, and then you shall set free the beautiful Princess Bride."

Said Angus: "Fain would I go forth at once to search for her."

"The wolf-month (February) has now come," the king said. "Uncertain is the temper of the wolf."

Said Angus: "I shall cast a spell on the sea and a spell on the land, and borrow for February three days from August."

He did as he said he would do. He borrowed

three days from August, and the ocean slumbered peacefully while the sun shone brightly over mountain and glen. Then Angus mounted his white steed and rode eastward to Scotland over the isles and over the Minch, and he reached the Grampians when dawn was breaking. He was clad in raiment of shining gold, and from his shoulders hung his royal robe of crimson which the wind uplifted and spread out in gleaming splendour athwart the sky.

An aged bard looked eastward, and when he beheld the fair Angus he lifted up his harp and sang a song of welcome, and the birds of the forest sang with him. And this is how he sang:—

> Angus hath come—the young, the fair,
> The blue-eyed god with golden hair—
> The god who to the world doth bring
> This morn the promise of the spring;
> Who moves the birds to song ere yet
> He hath awaked the violet,
> Or the soft primrose on the steep,
> While buds are laid in lidded sleep,
> And white snows wrap the hills serene,
> Ere glows the larch's [1] vivid green
> Through the brown woods and bare.   All hail!
> Angus, and may thy will prevail. . . .
> He comes . . . he goes. . . . And far and wide
> He searches for the Princess Bride.

Up and down the land went Angus, but he

[1] The larch is the first tree in Scotland which turns a bright green in springtime.

could not find Bride anywhere. The fair princess beheld him in a dream, however, and knew that he longed to set her free. When she awoke she shed tears of joy, and on the place where her tears fell there sprang up violets, and they were blue as her beautiful eyes.

Beira was angry when she came to know that Angus was searching for Bride, and on the third evening of his visit she raised a great tempest which drove him back to Green Isle. But he returned again and again, and at length he discovered the castle in which the princess was kept a prisoner.

Then came a day when Angus met Bride in a forest near the castle. The violets were blooming and soft yellow primroses opened their eyes of wonder to gaze on the prince and the princess. When they spoke one to another the birds raised their sweet voices in song and the sun shone fair and bright.

Said Angus: "Beautiful princess, I beheld you in a dream weeping tears of sorrow."

Bride said: "Mighty prince, I beheld you in a dream riding over bens and through glens in beauty and power."

Said Angus: "I have come to rescue you from Queen Beira, who has kept you all winter long in captivity."

Bride said: "To me this is a day of great joy."

Said Angus: " It will be a day of great joy to all mankind ever after this."

That is why the first day of spring—the day on which Angus found the princess—is called "Bride's Day".[1]

Through the forest came a fair company of fairy ladies, who hailed Bride as queen and bade welcome to Angus. Then the Fairy Queen waved her wand, and Bride was transformed. As swiftly as the bright sun springs out from behind a dark cloud, shedding beauty all round, so swiftly did Bride appear in new splendour. Instead of ragged clothing, she then wore a white robe adorned with spangles of shining silver. Over her heart gleamed a star-like crystal, pure as her thoughts and bright as the joy that Angus brought her. This gem is called "the guiding star of Bride". Her golden-brown hair, which hung down to her waist in gleaming curls, was decked with fair spring flowers—snowdrops and daisies and primroses and violets. Blue were her eyes, and her face had the redness and whiteness of the wild rose of peerless beauty and tender grace. In her right hand she carried a white wand entwined with golden corn-stalks, and in her left a golden horn which is called the " Horn of Plenty ".

The linnet was the first forest bird that hailed Bride in her beauty, and the Fairy Queen said:

---

[1] February 1st old style, February 13th new style.

"Ever after this you shall be called the 'Bird of Bride'." On the seashore the first bird that chirped with joy was the oyster-catcher, and the Fairy Queen said: "Ever after this you shall be called the 'Page of Bride'."

Then the Fairy Queen led Angus and Bride to her green-roofed underground palace in the midst of the forest. As they went forward they came to a river which was covered with ice. Bride put her fingers on the ice, and the Ice Hag shrieked and fled.

A great feast was held in the palace of the Fairy Queen, and it was the marriage feast of Bride, for Angus and she were wed. The fairies danced and sang with joy, and all the world was moved to dance and sing with them. This was how the first "Festival of Bride" came to be.

"Spring has come!" the shepherds cried; and they drove their flocks on to the moors, where they were counted and blessed.

"Spring has come!" chattered the raven, and flew off to find moss for her nest. The rook heard and followed after, and the wild duck rose from amidst the reeds, crying: "Spring has come!"

Bride came forth from the fairy palace with Angus and waved her hand, while Angus repeated magic spells. Then greater growth was given to the grass, and all the world hailed Angus and Bride as king and queen. Although they were not beheld by mankind, yet their presence was everywhere felt throughout Scotland.

Beira was wroth when she came to know that Angus had found Bride. She seized her magic hammer and smote the ground unceasingly until it was frozen hard as iron again—so hard that no herb or blade of grass could continue to live upon its surface. Terrible was her wrath when she beheld the grass growing. She knew well that when the grass flourished and Angus and Bride were married, her authority would pass away. It was her desire to keep her throne as long as possible.

"Bride is married, hail to Bride!" sang the birds.

"Angus is married, hail to Angus!" they sang also.

Beira heard the songs of the birds, and called to her hag servants: "Ride north and ride south, ride east and ride west, and wage war against Angus. I shall ride forth also."

Her servants mounted their shaggy goats and rode forth to do her bidding. Beira mounted a black steed and set out in pursuit of Angus. She rode fast and she rode hard. Black clouds swept over the sky as she rode on, until at length she came to the forest in which the Fairy Queen had her dwelling. All the fairies fled in terror into their green mound and the doors were shut.

Angus looked up and beheld Beira drawing nigh.
He leapt on the back of his white steed, and lifted
his young bride into the saddle in front of him
and fled away with her.

Angus rode westward over the hills and over
the valleys and over the sea, and Beira pursued
him.

There is a rocky ravine on the island of Tiree,
and Beira's black steed jumped across it while
pursuing the white steed of Angus. The hoofs
of the black steed made a gash on the rocks. To
this day the ravine is called " The Horse's Leap".

Angus escaped to the Green Isle of the West,
and there he passed happy days with Bride. But
he longed to return to Scotland and reign as King
of Summer. Again and again he crossed the
sea; and each time he reached the land of glens
and bens, the sun broke forth in brightness and
the birds sang merrily to welcome him.

Beira raised storm after storm to drive him
away. First she called on the wind named " The
Whistle ", which blew high and shrill, and brought
down rapid showers of cold hailstones. It lasted
for three days, and there was much sorrow and
bitterness throughout the length and breadth of
Scotland. Sheep and lambs were killed on the
moors, and horses and cows perished also.

Angus fled, but he returned soon again. The
next wind that Beira raised to prolong her winter

reign was the "Sharp Billed Wind" which is called "Gobag". It lasted for nine days, and all the land was pierced by it, for it pecked and bit in every nook and cranny like a sharp-billed bird.

Angus returned, and the Beira raised the eddy wind which is called "The Sweeper". Its whirling gusts tore branches from the budding trees and bright flowers from their stalks. All the time it blew, Beira kept beating the ground with her magic hammer so as to keep the grass from growing. But her efforts were in vain. Spring smiled in beauty all around, and each time she turned away, wearied by her efforts, the sun sprang forth in splendour. The small modest primroses opened their petals in the sunshine, looking forth from cosy nooks that the wind, called "Sweeper", was unable to reach. Angus fled, but he soon returned again.

Beira was not yet, however, entirely without hope. Her efforts had brought disaster to mankind, and the "Weeks of Leanness" came on. Food became scarce. The fishermen were unable to venture to sea on account of Beira's tempests, and could get no fish. In the night-time Beira and her hags entered the dwellings of mankind, and stole away their stores of food. It was, indeed, a sorrowful time.

Angus was moved with pity for mankind, and tried to fight the hags of Beira. But the fierce queen raised the "Gales of Complaint" to keep him away, and they raged in fury until the first week of March. Horses and cattle died for want of food, because the fierce winds blew down stacks of fodder and scattered them over the lochs and the ocean.

Angus, however, waged a fierce struggle against the hag servants, and at length he drove them away to the north, where they fumed and fretted furiously.

Beira was greatly alarmed, and she made her last great effort to subdue the Powers of Spring. She waved her magic hammer, and smote the clouds with it. Northward she rode on her black steed, and gathered her servants together, and called to them, saying: " Ride southward with me, all of you, and scatter our enemies before us."

Out of the bleak dark north they rode in a single pack. With them came the Big Black Tempest. It seemed then as if winter had returned in full strength and would abide for ever. But even Beira and her hags had to take rest. On a dusky evening they crouched down together on the side of a bare mountain, and, when they did so, a sudden calm fell upon the land and the sea.

" Ha! ha!" laughed the wild duck who hated the hag. " Ha! ha! I am still alive, and so are my six ducklings."

"Have patience! idle chatterer," answered the Hag. "I am not yet done."

That night she borrowed three days from Winter which had not been used, for Angus had previously borrowed for Winter three days from August. The three spirits of the borrowed days were tempest spirits, and came towards Beira mounted on black hogs. She spoke to them, saying: "Long have you been bound! Now I set you at liberty."

One after another, on each of the three days that followed, the spirits went forth riding the black hogs. They brought snow and hail and fierce blasts of wind. Snow whitened the moors and filled the furrows of ploughed land, rivers rose in flood, and great trees were shattered and uprooted. The duck was killed, and so were her six ducklings; sheep and cattle perished, and many human beings were killed on land and drowned at sea. The days on which these things happened are called the "Three Hog Days".

Beira's reign was now drawing to a close. She found herself unable to combat any longer against the power of the new life that was rising in every vein of the land. The weakness of extreme old age crept upon her, and she longed once again to drink of the waters of the Well of Youth. When, on a bright March morning, she beheld Angus riding over the hills on his white steed, scattering her fierce hag servants before him, she fled away in despair. Ere she went she threw her magic hammer beneath a holly tree, and that is the reason why no grass grows under the holly trees.

Beira's black steed went northward with her in flight. As it leapt over Loch Etive it left the marks of its hoofs on the side of a rocky mountain, and the spot is named to this day "Horse-shoes". She did not rein up her steed until she reached the island of Skye, where she found rest on the summit of the "Old Wife's Ben" (Ben-e-Cail-lich) at Broadford. There she sat, gazing stead-fastly across the sea, waiting until the day and night would be of equal length. All that equal day she wept tears of sorrow for her lost power, and when night came on she went westward over the sea to Green Island. At the dawn of the day that followed she drank the magic waters of the Well of Youth.

On that day which is of equal length with the night, Angus came to Scotland with Bride, and they were hailed as king and queen of the unseen beings. They rode from south to north in the morning and forenoon, and from north to south in the afternoon and evening. A gentle wind went with them, blowing towards the north from dawn till midday, and towards the south from midday till sunset.

It was on that day that Bride dipped her fair white hands in the high rivers and lochs which still retained ice. When she did so, the Ice Hag fell into a deep sleep from which she could not awake until summer and autumn were over and past.

The grass grew quickly after Angus began to reign as king. Seeds were sown, and the people called on Bride to grant them a good harvest. Ere long the whole land was made beautiful with spring flowers of every hue.

Angus had a harp of gold with silver strings, and when he played on it youths and maidens followed the sound of the music through the woods. Bards sang his praises and told that he kissed lovers, and that when they parted one from another to return to their homes, the kisses became invisible birds that hovered round their heads and sang sweet songs of love, and whispered memories dear. It was thus that one bard sang of him:—

> When softly blew the south wind o'er the sea,
> Lisping of springtime hope and summer pride,
> And the rough reign of Beira ceased to be,
>   Angus the Ever-Young,
> The beauteous god of love, the golden-haired,
>   The blue mysterious-eyed,
> Shone like the star of morning high among
>   The stars that shrank afraid
> When dawn proclaimed the triumph that he shared

With Bride the peerless maid.
Then winds of violet sweetness rose and sighed,
No conquest is compared
To Love's transcendent joys that never fade.

In the old days, when there was no Calendar in Scotland, the people named the various periods of winter and spring, storm and calm, as they are given above. The story of the struggle between Angus and Beira is the story of the struggle between spring and winter, growth and decay, light and darkness, and warmth and cold.

CHAPTER III

Combats that Never End

There are two mountains that overlook the Spey valley, one to the east and one to the west, and a fairy king dwells on each of them. They are both sons of Beira. One fairy king is white, and has great fame as an archer; he has a silver bow and arrows of gold, and once a day he shoots an arrow across the strath. The other fairy king is black as the raven, and on his left breast there is a red spot. He has no weapon, but is yet terrible in battle, because he can make himself invisible at will. When he does so, nothing remains in sight except the red spot. He has great strength, and when he goes against his enemies he seizes them unawares and throws them to the ground. No matter how well they are armed, his enemies tremble when the invisible fairy comes against them. All they see is a red spot moving about in the air.

Now, the white fairy has a fair bride whose name is Face-of-Light. It is a great joy to her to wander among the mountains where herds of

deer crop the green herbage, and through the
strath where cornfields rustle in soft winds and
fragrant flowers bloom fair to see. The black
fairy has no bride, and is jealous of the white fairy
because his days are filled with joy by the beauty
of Face-of-Light. These two fairies have ever
been enemies. The black fairy keeps out of sight
of the famous archer, fearing his arrows of gold.

One summer evening when the twilight shadows
were lengthening and deepening across the strath,
Face of Light tripped merrily over the grassy
banks, gathering wild flowers. Silence had fallen
on the world; no bird sang and no wind whispered,
the lochs were asleep, and the shrunken river
made scarcely a sound louder than the sigh of a
sleeping babe; it was no longer bright when
Face-of-Light turned away from it.

The black fairy looked out from his mountain
home. He knew that the white fairy had lain
down to rest, and he watched Face-of-Light
gathering wild flowers. Nearer and nearer she
came to his dwelling, and he crept into a deep
forest which conceals the entrance to his mountain, and waited to seize her. Face-of-Light,
never dreaming of her peril, tripped towards the
edge of the forest; and, seeing many flowers
growing beneath the trees, went in to pluck them.
She made the forest bright with her beauty, and
the flowers grew fairer as she drew near them.

Suddenly a great black hand was thrust out from a thick clump of bushes. The hand seized her, and she shrieked in terror and struggled to escape. The white fairy heard her cries, which pierced the air like the keen long whistle of the curlew, leapt up, and looked forth from his mountain top. In a moment he knew what had happened. Face-of-Light had been seized by his enemy, the black fairy, who was dragging her to a dark dungeon in the middle of his mountain. The white fairy was unable to go to her rescue for two reasons. Like his dark enemy, he could not pass the utmost limits of his mountain house, and having already shot a golden arrow that day, he could not shoot another until a new day had dawned.

Night came on, and the black fairy climbed to the top of his mountain, where he danced with joy because he had taken captive the bride of his enemy. The white fairy was stricken with sorrow, and when he heard the cries of Face-of-Light coming from the dungeon, he fell down in a swoon.

All night long Face-of-Light sobbed and wept, while the black fairy danced on the mountain top and sang songs of triumph. He danced so fast that he raised a wind which swept down the strath and shook the trees from sleep, so that they moaned and sighed all night long. The cries of Face-of-Light were heard by human beings, and those who were awakened said one to another: "Listen to the hag of night. How terrible are her cries!"

Not until the dawn began to break did the white fairy recover from his swoon. Just when the first shaft of grey light pierced the eastern sky, he opened his eyes. Then he remembered his sorrow and wept softly. His tears fell as dew on the flowers and the grass.

Weeping, he climbed his mountain, and then wandered round about the crest of it. His heart was heavy for the loss of Face-of-Light, and when he listened he heard her moaning in her dark prison. The black fairy had ceased to dance. He stood upright on the highest point of his mountain house, and shouted to his enemy: "Ha! Face-of-Light is my prisoner." Then suddenly he was silent He saw the white fairy stringing his silver bow and then drawing from his shining quiver a bright golden arrow.

"Ha!" cried the black fairy, "would you dare shoot at me?"

"Set free Face-of-Light, or I shall shoot," the white fairy made answer. His face was white as snow and hard as ice.

The black fairy laughed, and willed himself to become invisible, and then, just as the white fairy raised his bow to take aim, his enemy vanished from sight. No part of him could be seen but the great red spot on his left breast, which seemed to float in the air.

For a moment the white fairy, gazing eastward, looked with wonder at the red spot which grew brighter and brighter. His bow was bent, and his golden arrow was held ready for flight.

The sound of defiant laughter came down the wind as the black fairy, now invisible, danced with joy on his mountain top.

To and fro swayed the red spot, and the white fairy thought he would shoot at it. His aim was true and his arm was strong. Straight from the bow flew the bright golden arrow. It darted through the air with lightning speed and struck the red spot, which, be it known, was the heart of the black fairy. A shriek rang out across the strath. It was the death shriek of the black fairy, who fell down on the bare rock and died. His life-blood streamed forth, and the whole eastern sky was covered with it. In the midst of the redness gleamed the bright golden arrow of the white fairy.

No sooner was the black fairy slain than Face-of-Light was set free. The doors of her dungeon flew open, and she came forth in all her beauty. When she did so, the mountains and the strath were made bright, the river sparkled in the light, and the lochs flashed like burnished silver. All the land was made glad when Face-of-Light was

set free from her dark prison. The slumbering
flowers opened their eyes to gaze upon her, and
the birds broke forth in merry song, while the
white fairy smiled and danced with joy.

The black fairy lay dead and invisible on his
mountain top until evening came on. Then Beira
came to visit him. When she found that her son
had been slain, she took from her wallet a pot of
healing balsam and rubbed it on his wound. Then
she rubbed the balsam on his eyes and on his lips.
When she did this, he came to life, and began
once again to plot evil against the white fairy and
his beautiful bride.

This story, which used to be told in Strathspey,
is the story of the struggle between darkness and
light. The black fairy is night, which begins to
make itself invisible at dawn, and the red spot on
his left breast is the red light of morning. The
golden arrow of the white fairy is the golden shaft
of sunlight that darts across the eastern heaven
as the sun rises in morning splendour. Face-of-
Light is the spirit of the River Spey, which is
bright in daytime and lost to sight in the darkness of night. When the story-teller says that
Face-of-Light leaves the river, he means that its
brightness leaves it when the shadows of night
are falling.

A different story is told in the Ness valley.
There are two mountains on either side of Loch

Ness, and on each is a Fooar, or giant. These sons of Beira are rivals. One loves the daylight and the other loves darkness.

Every morning at dawn one Fooar flings across Loch Ness a white boulder. When the boulder goes through the air the sky becomes bright. Every evening the other Fooar flings across Loch Ness a black boulder, and the sky grows dark.

The rivals can throw their boulders only once in every twenty-four hours. When the white boulder is flung, it strikes the night Fooar, and he falls down in a swoon. He does not recover until evening, and then he rises and, in turn, flings his black boulder, and strikes down his rival, who then lies unconscious until the dawn. When the giant of day grasps his white boulder and raises it on high, his red hand can be seen in the sky, and the red hand of the giant of night is often seen at evening. Sometimes the giants turn round the boulders to adjust them for throwing. Then the gold rings on their fingers and the golden armlets on their arms flash athwart the sky in bright splendour.

CHAPTER IV

The Princess of Land-under-Waves

When no wind blows and the surface of the sea is clear as crystal, the beauties of Land-under-Waves are revealed to human eyes. It is a fair country with green vales through which flow silvern streams, and the pebbles in the beds of the streams are flashing gems of varied hues. There are deep forests that glitter in eternal sunshine, and bright flowers that never fade. Rocks are of gold, and the sand is dust of silver.

On a calm morning in May, the Feans, who were great warriors in ancient Scotland, being the offspring of gods and goddesses, were sitting beside the Red Cataract, below which salmon moved slowly, resting themselves ere they began to leap towards the higher waters of the stream. The sun was shining bright, and the sea was without a ripple. With eyes of wonder the Feans gazed on the beauties of Land-under-Waves. None spoke, so deeply were they absorbed. They saw the silver sands, the rocks of gold, the gleam-

ing forests, the beautiful flowers, and the bright
streams that flow over beds covered with flashing
gems.

As they gazed a boat was seen on the sea, and
for a time the Feans were not sure whether it
moved above the surface or below it. In time,
however, as it drew near they saw that it was on
the surface. The boat came towards the place
where they sat, and they saw that a woman pulled
the oars.

All the Feans rose to their feet. Finn, the
King of the Feans, and Goll, his chief warrior,
had keen sight, and when the boat was still afar
off they saw that the woman had great beauty.
She pulled two oars, which parted the sea, and
the ripples seemed to set in motion all the trees
and flowers of Land-under-Waves.

The boat came quickly, and when it grounded
on the beach, the loveliest woman that ever eyes
gazed upon rose out of it. Her face was mild
and touched with a soft sadness. She was a
stranger to the Feans, who knew well that she
had come from afar, and they wondered whence
she came and what were the tidings she brought.

The young woman walked towards Finn and
saluted him, and for a time Finn and all the
Feans were made silent by her exceeding great
beauty. At length Finn spoke to her. "You
are welcome, fair young stranger," he said. "Tell

us what tribe you are from, and what is the purpose of your journey to the land of the Feans."

Softly spoke the young woman, saying: "I am the daughter of King Under-Waves, and I shall tell you why I have come here. There is not a land beneath the sun which I have not searched for Finn and his brave warriors."

"Beautiful maiden," Finn said, "will you not tell us why you have searched through the lands that are far and near, seeking to find us?"

"Then you are Finn and no other," spoke the maiden.

"I am indeed Finn, and these who stand near me are my warriors." It was thus that Finn made answer, speaking modestly, and yet not without pride.

"I have come to ask for your help," said the maiden, "and I shall have need of it very soon. Mine enemy pursues me even now."

"I promise to help you, fair princess," Finn assured her. "Tell me who it is that pursues you."

Said the maiden: "He who pursues me over the ocean is a mighty and fearless warrior. His name is Dark Prince-of-Storm, and he is the son of the White King of Red-Shields. He means to seize the kingdom of my father and make me his bride. I have defied him, saying: 'Finn shall take me to my home; he shall be my saviour.

Great as is your prowess, you cannot fight and beat Finn and his heroic band.'"

Oscar, the young hero and the grandson of Finn, spoke forth and said: " Even if Finn were not here, the Dark Prince would not dare to seize you."

As he spoke a shadow fell athwart the sea, blotting out the vision of Land-under-Waves. The Feans looked up, and they saw on the sky-line a mighty warrior mounted on a blue-grey steed of ocean; white was its mane and white its tail, and white the foam that was driven from its nostrils and its mouth.

The warrior came swiftly towards the shore, and as his steed rode forward with great fury, waves rose and broke around it.   The breath from its panting nostrils came over the sea like gusts of tempest.

On the warrior's head was a flashing helmet, and on his left arm a ridged shield.   In his right hand he grasped a large heavy sword, and when he waved it on high it flashed bright like lightning.

Faster than a mountain torrent galloped his horse.   The Feans admired the Dark Prince. He was a great and mighty warrior who bore himself like a king.

The steed came to land, and when it did so, the Dark Prince leapt from its back and strode up the beach.

Finn spoke to the fair daughter of the King Under-Waves and said: "Is this the prince of whom you have spoken?"

Said the princess: "It is he and no other. Oh, protect me now, for great is his power!"

"Goll, the old warrior, and Oscar, the youthful hero, sprang forward and placed themselves between the Dark Prince and the fair princess. But the Dark Prince scorned to combat with him. He went towards Finn, who was unarmed. Goll was made angry at once. He seized a spear and flung it at the stranger. It did not touch his body, but it split the ridged shield right through the middle. Then Oscar raised his spear and flung it from his left hand. It struck the warrior's steed and slew it. This was accounted a mighty deed, and Ossian,[1] the bard of the Feans, and father of Oscar, celebrated it in a song which is still sung in Scotland.

When the steed perished, Dark Prince turned round with rage and fury, and called for fifty heroes to combat against him. Then he said that he would overcome all the Feans and take away the fair princess.

A great battle was waged on the beach. The Dark Prince sprang upon the Feans, and fought with fierceness and great strength.

At length Goll went against him. Both fought

[1] Pronounced Osh'yan in Scottish Gaelic.

with their swords alone, and never was seen before such a furious combat. Strong was the arm of Goll, and cunning the thrusts he gave. As he fought on, his battle power increased, and at length he struck down and slew the Dark Prince. Nor was ever such a hero overcome since the day when the Ocean Giant was slain.

When the Dark Prince was slain, the wind fell and the sea was hushed, and the sun at evening shone over the waters. Once again Land-under-Waves was revealed in all its beauty.

The princess bade farewell to all the Feans, and Finn went into a boat and went with her across the sea until they reached the gates of Land-under-Waves. The entrance to this wonderful land is a sea-cave on the Far Blue Isle of Ocean. When Finn took leave of the princess, she made him promise that if ever she had need of his help again, he would give it to her freely and quickly.

A year and a day went past, and then came a calm and beautiful morning. Once again the Feans sat on the shore below the Red Cataract, gazing on the beauties of Land-under-Waves. As they gazed, a boat came over the sea, and there was but one person in it.

Said Oscar: "Who comes hither? Is it the princess of Land-under-Waves once more?"

Finn looked seaward and said: "No, it is not the princess who comes hither, but a young man."

The boat drew swiftly towards the shore, and when the man was within call he hailed Finn with words of greeting and praise.

"Who are you, and whence come you?" Finn asked.

Said the man: "I am the messenger of the princess of Land-under-Waves. She is ill, and seems ready to die."

There was great sorrow among the Feans when they heard the sad tidings.

"What is your message from the fair princess?" Finn asked.

Said the man: "She bids you to remember your promise to help her in time of need."

"I have never forgotten my promise," Finn told him, "and am ready now to fulfil it."

Said the man: "Then ask Jeermit, the healer, to come with me so that he may give healing to the Princess Under-Waves."

Finn made a sign to Jeermit, and he rose up and went down the beach and entered the boat. Then the boat went out over the sea towards the Far Blue Isle, and it went swiftly until it reached the sea-cave through which one must pass to enter Land-under-Waves.

Now Jeermit was the fairest of all the members of the Fean band. His father was Angus-the-Ever-Young, who conferred upon him the power to give healing for wounds and sickness. Jeermit had knowledge of curative herbs and life-giving waters, and he had the power, by touching a sufferer, to prolong life until he found the means to cure.

Jeermit was taken through the sea-cave of the Far Blue Isle, and for a time he saw naught, so thick was the darkness; but he heard the splashing of waves against the rocks. At length light broke forth, and the boat grounded. Jeermit stepped out, and found himself on a broad level plain. The boatman walked in front, and Jeermit followed him. They went on and on, and it seemed that their journey would never end. Jeermit saw a clump of red sphagnum moss, and plucked some and went on. Ere long he saw another clump, and plucked some more. A third time he came to a red moss clump, and from it too he plucked a portion. The boatman still led on and on, yet Jeermit never felt weary.

At length Jeermit saw before him a golden castle. He spoke to the boatman, saying: "Whose castle is that?"

Said the boatman: "It is the castle of King Under-Waves, and the princess lies within."

Jeermit entered the castle. He saw many courtiers with pale faces. None spoke: all were hushed to silence with grief. The queen came towards him, and she seized his right hand and led him towards the chamber in which the dying princess lay.

Jeermit knelt beside her, and when he touched her the power of his healing entered her veins, and she opened her eyes. As soon as she beheld Jeermit of the Feans she smiled a sweet smile, and all who were in the chamber smiled too.

"I feel stronger already," the princess told Jeermit. "Great is the joy I feel to behold you. But the sickness has not yet left me, and I fear I shall die."

"I have three portions of red moss," said Jeermit. "If you will take them in a drink they will heal you, because they are the three life drops of your heart."

"Alas!" the princess exclaimed, "I cannot drink of any water now except from the cup of the King of the Plain of Wonder."

Now, great as was Jeermit's knowledge, he had never heard before of this magic cup.

"A wise woman has told that if I get three draughts from this cup I shall be cured," said the princess. "She said also that when I drink I must swallow the three portions of red moss from the Wide-Bare-Plain. The moss of healing you have already found, O Jeermit. But no man shall ever gain possession of the magic cup of the King of the Plain-of-Wonder, and I shall not therefore get it, and must die."

Said Jeermit: "There is not in the world above the sea, or the world below the sea, a single man who will keep the cup from me.   Tell me where dwells the King of the Plain-of-Wonder.   Is his palace far distant from here?"

"No, it is not far distant," the princess told him.   "Plain-of-Wonder is the next kingdom to that of my father.   The two kingdoms are divided by a river.   You may reach that river, O Jeermit, but you may never be able to cross it."

Said Jeermit: "I now lay healing spells upon you, and you shall live until I return with the magic cup."

When he had spoken thus, he rose up and walked out of the castle.   The courtiers who had been sad when he entered were merry as he went away, and those who had been silent spoke one to another words of comfort and hope, because Jeermit had laid healing spells upon the princess.

The King and the Queen of Land-under-Waves bade the healer of the Feans farewell, and wished him a safe and speedy journey.

Jeermit went on alone in the direction of the Plain-of-Wonder.   He went on and on until he reached the river of which the princess had spoken.   Then he walked up and down the river bank searching for a ford, but he could not find one.

"I cannot cross over," he said aloud.   "The princess has spoken truly."

As he spoke a little brown man rose up out of

the river. "Jeermit," he said, "you are now in sore straits."

Said Jeermit: "Indeed I am. You have spoken wisely."

"What would you give to one who would help you in your trouble?"

"Whatever he may ask of me."

"All I ask for," said the brown man, "is your goodwill."

"That you get freely," said Jeermit to him.

"I shall carry you across the river," said the little man.

"You cannot do that."

"Yes, indeed I can."

He stretched forth his hands and took Jeermit on his back, and walked across the river with him, treading the surface as if it were hard ground.

As they crossed the river they passed an island over which hovered a dark mist.

"What island is that?" asked Jeermit.

"Its name," the brown man told him, "is Cold Isle-of-the-Dead. There is a well on the island, and the water of it is healing water."

They reached the opposite bank, and the brown man said: "You are going to the palace of King Ian of Wonder-Plain."

"I am."

"You desire to obtain the Cup of Healing."

"That is true."

"May you get it," said the brown man, who thereupon entered the river.

Ere he disappeared he spoke again and said: "Know you where you now are?"

"In the Kingdom of Plain-of-Wonder," Jeermit said.

"That is true," said the little brown man. "It is also Land-under-Mountains. This river divides Land-under-Mountains from Land-under-Waves."

Jeermit was about to ask a question, but ere he could speak the little brown man vanished from before his eyes.

Jeermit went on and on. There was no sun above him and yet all the land was bright. No darkness ever comes to Land-under-Mountains, and there is no morning there and no evening, but always endless day.

Jeermit went on and on until he saw a silver castle with a roof of gleaming crystal. The doors were shut, and guarded by armed warriors.

Jeermit blew a blast on his horn, and called out, "Open and let me in."

A warrior went towards him with drawn sword. Jeermit flung his spear and slew the warrior.

Then the doors of the castle were opened and King Ian came forth.

"Who are you, and whence come you?" he asked sternly.

"I am Jeermit," was the answer he received.

"Son of Angus-the-Ever-Young, you are welcome," exclaimed the king. "Why did you not send a message that you were coming? It is sorrowful to think you have slain my greatest warrior."

Said Jeermit: "Give him to drink of the water in the Cup of Healing."

"Bring forth the cup!" the king called.

The cup was brought forth, and the king gave it to Jeermit, saying: "There is no virtue in the cup unless it is placed in hands of either Angus or his son."

Jeermit touched the slain warrior's lips with the cup. He poured drops of the water into the man's mouth, and he sat up. Then he drank all the water in the cup, and rose to his feet strong and well again, for his wound had been healed.

Said Jeermit to the king: "I have come hither to obtain this cup, and will now take it with me and go away."

"So be it," answered the king. "I give you the cup freely. But remember that there is no longer any healing in it, for my mighty warrior has drunk the magic water."

Jeermit was not too well pleased when the King of Wonder-Plain spoke thus. "No matter," said he; "I shall take the cup with me."

"I will send a boat to take you across the river and past the Cold-Isle-of-the-Dead," the king said.

Said Jeermit: "I thank you, but I have no need of a boat."

"May you return soon," the King said with a smile, for he believed that Jeermit would never be able to cross the river or pass the Cold-Isle-of-the-Dead.

Jeermit bade the king farewell and went away, as he had come, all alone. He went on and on until he reached the river. Then he sat down, and gloomy thoughts entered his mind. He had obtained the cup, but it was empty: he had returned to the river and could not cross it.

"Alas!" he exclaimed aloud, "my errand is fruitless. The cup is of no use to me, and I cannot cross the river, and must needs return in shame to the King of Wonder-Plain."

As he spoke the little brown man rose out of the river.

"You are again in sore straits, Jeermit," he said.

"Indeed, I am," answered the son of Angus. "I got what I went for, but it is useless, and I cannot cross the river."

"I shall carry you," said the little brown man.

"So be it," Jeermit answered.

The little brown man walked over the river with Jeermit on his shoulders, and went towards the Cold-Isle-of-the-Dead.

"Whither are you carrying me now?" asked Jeermit with fear in his heart.

Said the little brown man: "You desire to heal the daughter of King Under-Waves."

"That is true."

"Your cup is empty, and you must fill it at the Well of Healing, on the Cold-Isle-of-the-Dead. That is why I am carrying you towards the isle. You must not get off my back or set foot on the shore, else you will never be able to leave it. But have no fear. I shall kneel down beside the well, and you can dip the cup in it, and carry off enough water to heal the princess."

Jeermit was well pleased to hear these words, for he knew that the little brown man was indeed his friend. He obtained the healing water in the manner that was promised. Then the little brown man carried him to the opposite bank of the river, and set him down on the border of Land-under-Waves.

"Now you are happy-hearted," said the little brown man.

"Happy-hearted indeed," Jeermit answered.

"Ere I bid you farewell I shall give you good advice," said the little brown man.

"Why have you helped me as you have done?" Jeermit asked.

"Because your heart is warm, and you desire to do good to others," said the little brown man. "Men who do good to others will ever find friends in the Land of the Living, in the Land of the

Dead, in Land-under-Waves, and in Land-under-Mountains."

"I thank you," Jeermit said. "Now I am ready for your good advice, knowing that your friendship is true and lasting."

Said the little brown man: "You may give the princess water from the Cup-of-Healing, but she will not be cured unless you drop into the water three portions of sphagnum moss."

"I have already found these portions on the broad level plain."

"That is well," said the other. "Now I have more advice to offer you. When the princess is healed the king will offer you choice of reward. Take no thing he offers, but ask for a boat to convey you home again."

"I will follow your advice," Jeermit promised.

Then the two parted, and Jeermit went on and on until he came to the golden palace of King Under-Waves. The princess welcomed him when he was brought into her room, and said: "No man ever before was given the cup you now carry."

Said Jeermit: "For your sake I should have got it, even if I had to fight an army."

"I feared greatly that you would never return," sighed the princess.

Jeermit put into the Cup-of-Healing the three portions of blood-red moss which he had found, and bade the princess to drink.

THE CUP OF HEALING

From a drawing by John Duncan, A.R.S.A.

Thrice she drank, and each time she swallowed a portion of red moss. When she drank the last drop, having swallowed the third portion of red moss, she said: "Now I am healed. Let a feast be made ready, and I shall sit at the board with you."

There was great joy and merriment in the castle when the feast was held. Sorrow was put away, and music was sounded. When the feast was over, the king spoke to Jeermit and said: "I would fain reward you for healing my daughter, the princess. I shall give you as much silver and gold as you desire, and you shall marry my daughter and become the heir to my throne."

Said Jeermit: "If I marry your daughter I cannot again return to my own land."

"No, you cannot again return, except on rare and short visits. But here you will spend happy days, and everyone shall honour you."

Said Jeermit: "The only reward I ask for, O king, is a small one indeed."

"I promise to give you whatever you ask for."

Said Jeermit: "Give me a boat, so that I may return again to my own land, which is very dear to me, and to my friends and kinsmen, the Feans, whom I love, and to Finn mac Cool, the great chief of men."

"Your wish is granted," the king said.

Then Jeermit bade farewell to all who were in

the castle, and when he parted with the princess she said: "I shall never forget you, Jeermit. You found me in suffering and gave me relief; you found me dying and gave me back my life again. When you return to your own land remember me, for I shall never pass an hour of life without thinking of you with joy and thankfulness."

Jeermit crossed the level plain once again, and reached the place where the boat in which he had come lay safely moored. The boatman went into it and seized the oars, and Jeermit went in after him. Then the boat sped through the deep dark tunnel, where the waves splash unseen against the rocks, and passed out of the cave on the shore of Far-Blue-Isle. The boat then went speedily over the sea, and while it was yet afar off, Finn saw it coming. All the Feans gathered on the shore to bid Jeermit welcome.

"Long have we waited for you, son of Angus," Finn said.

"What time has passed since I went away?" asked Jeermit, for it seemed to him that he had been absent for no more than a day and a night.

"Seven long years have passed since we bade you farewell," Finn told him, "and we feared greatly that you would never again come back to us."

Said Jeermit: "In the lands I visited there is

no night, and no change in the year.   Glad am I
to return home once again."

Then they all went to Finn's house, and a great
feast was held in honour of Jeermit, who brought
back with him the Cup-of-Healing which he had
received from the King of Wonder-Plain.

CHAPTER V

Nimble Men, Blue Men, and Green Ladies

Among the children and descendants of Beira are the Nimble Men, or Merry Dancers (Aurora Borealis), the Blue Men of the Minch, and the Green Ladies.

The Nimble Men are divided into two clans. The heroes of one clan are clad in garments white as hoar-frost, and the heroes of the other clan in garments of pale yellow. Brighter and more varied colours are worn by the ladies of the clans. Some are gowned in green, some in red, and some in silvery white, and a few wear royal purple.

On winter nights when there is peace on land and sea the Nimble Men and Merry Maidens come forth to dance in the northern sky. They are all of giant stature but comely of form, and their dances are very graceful. The men bow to the maids and the maids curtsy to the men, and when the dance is at its height some of the men leap high and whirl round about, so merry do they become. Fairy pipers play enchanting music while the merry couples dance across the northern sky.

There was once a prince of the White Clan of
Nimble Men, and his name was Light Foot. He
loved the Princess Comely, who was the fairest
of all the Merry Maidens, and he had a rival
named Green Eyes, the chief of the Yellow Clan.
Princess Comely liked best to dance with Light
Foot, because among the Nimble Men he was
without an equal as a dancer.

One dark night when the mountains were white
with new-fallen snow and the valleys glistened
with hoar-frost, all the northern sky was lit up in
splendour by the Nimble Men and Merry Maidens,
who came out to dance in honour of Queen Beira.
It was the first great gathering of the winter
season, and all the dancers were clad in new
and dazzling garments. They began to dance
soon after darkness set in, and it was nigh to
midnight ere they sank down to rest.

Princess Comely had danced all the time with
Light Foot, and when she sat down he knelt
before her, whispering softly: " Fairest of the fair,
O be my bride!"

Said Princess Comely: " Your bride I shall be."

The words were heard by Green Eyes, who
was crouching near at hand. His heart was filled
with anger, and, leaping up, he called upon the
members of his clan to draw their swords and
fight Light Foot and his followers. Then all was
confusion. The warriors of both clans sprang at

one another, brandishing their gleaming weapons. Up leapt Light Foot to fight against Green Eyes. Rising to full stature he darted across the sky to smite him down.   Up leapt the Princess Comely and all the maidens, and ran away shrieking. Then a battle royal began to rage between the rival clans.   The sound of swords striking swords reached the earth, and seemed like the rustling of frosty twigs when the wind rises suddenly and scampers through the forest.

For hours the fearsome fight was waged with fury, and men and women came forth to watch it with wonder and in silence.   They saw the warriors leaping white with anger.   Hard and swift were the blows, and many were slain.   At length below the feet of the Nimble Men there appeared a cloud which was red with the blood that flowed from many wounds received in the battle royal. From the sky the blood drops fell like dew on the green stones of the mountain, which were thus for ever stained with red spots.   That is why the red-speckled green stones are called "blood stones".

When the night was almost spent, Princess Comely returned to the battle-ground, and found that the conflict had come to an end.   As she drew near, a few wounded warriors rose up and staggered away.   She began to search among the fallen warriors for Light Foot, and at length she found him lying cold and dead.   A cry of sorrow

broke from her lips, and was wafted towards the
earth on the first breath of dawn. Those who
heard it knew then that the prophecy of the Seer
was being fulfilled, and they sang the song he
had made:—

> When yon lady seeks her lover
> In the cold and pearly morn,
> She will find that he has fallen
> By the hand that she did scorn.
> She will clasp her arms about him
> And in her anguish die—
> Oh, never again will trip the twain across the Northern Sky!

The Blue Men are found only in the Minch, and
chiefly in the strait which lies between the Island
of Lewis and the Shant Isles (the charmed islands),
and is called the " Sea-stream of the Blue Men".
They are not giants, like the Nimble Men, but of
human size, and they have great strength. By
day and by night they swim round and between
the Shant Isles, and the sea there is never at rest.
The Blue Men wear blue caps and have grey
faces which appear above the waves that they
raise with their long restless arms. In summer
weather they skim lightly below the surface, but
when the wind is high they revel in the storm
and swim with heads erect, splashing the waters
with mad delight. Sometimes they are seen
floating from the waist out of the sea, and sometimes turning round like porpoises as they dive.

Here is a boatman's song about the Blue Men:

When the tide is at the turning and the wind is fast asleep,
And not a wave is curling on the wide, blue deep,
Oh, the waters will be churning in the stream that never smiles,
Where the Blue Men are splashing round the charmèd isles.

As the summer wind goes droning o'er the sun-bright seas,
And the Minch is all a-dazzle to the Hebrides,
They will skim along like salmon—you can see their shoulders
    gleam,
And the flashing of their fingers in the Blue Men's Stream.

But when the blast is raving and the wild tide races,
The Blue Men are breast-high with foam-grey faces;
They'll plunge along with fury while they sweep the spray
    behind,
Oh, they'll bellow o'er the billows and wail upon the wind.

And if my boat be storm-toss'd and beating for the bay,
They'll be howling and be growling as they drench it with the
    spray—
For they'd like to heel it over to their laughter when it lists,
Or crack the keel between them, or stave it with their fists.

Oh, weary on the Blue Men, their anger and their wiles!
The whole day long, the whole night long, they're splashing
    round the isles;
They'll follow every fisher—ah! they'll haunt the fisher's
    dream—
When billows toss, Oh, who would cross the Blue Men's Stream!

In days of old the " Blue Men's Stream " was
sometimes called " The Current of Destruction ",
because so many ships were swamped in it.   The
people blamed the Blue Men, who dwelt in caves,

they said, at the bottom of the sea. Their
sentinels were always on the look-out, and when
a vessel came in sight, word was sent to the men
in the caves to come up. Sailors were afraid of
them, and many sailed round the Shant Islands
instead of taking the short cut between these
and the big Island of Lewis.

When the chief of the Blue Men had all his
men gathered about him, ready to attack a ship,
he rose high in the water and shouted to the
skipper two lines of poetry, and if the skipper did
not reply at once by adding two lines to complete
the verse, the Blue Men seized the ship and upset
it. Many a ship was lost in days of old because
the skipper had no skill at verse.

True is the Gaelic saying, however: "There
comes with time what comes not with weather".

One day, when the wind was high and the
billows rough and angry, the Blue Men saw a
stately ship coming towards their sea-stream under
white sails. Royally she cleft her way through
the waves. The sentinels called to the blue
fellows who were on the sea floor, and as they
rose they wondered to see the keel pass overhead so swiftly. Some seized it and shook it as
if to try their strength, and were astonished to
find it so steady and heavy. It carried on straight
as a spear in flight.

The chief of the Blue Men bobbed up in front

of the ship, and, when waist-high among the
tumbling waves, shouted to the skipper:—

> Man of the black cap, what do you say
> As your proud ship cleaves the brine?

No sooner were the words spoken than the
skipper answered:—

> My speedy ship takes the shortest way,
> And I'll follow you line by line.

This was at once an answer and a challenge,
and the chief of the Blue Men cried angrily:—

> My men are eager, my men are ready
> To drag you below the waves—

The skipper answered defiantly in a loud voice:

> My ship is speedy, my ship is steady,
> If it sank it would wreck your caves.

The chief of the Blue Men was worsted. Never
before had a seaman answered him so promptly
and so well. He had no power to injure the ship,
because the skipper was as good a bard as he was
himself, and he knew that if he went on shouting
half-verses until the storm spent itself the skipper
would always complete them. He signalled to
his followers to dive; and down below the wave
ridges they all vanished, like birds that dive for
fish. The big ship went on proudly and safely
under snow-white, wind-tight sails while—

> The sea-wind through the cordage sang
> With high and wintry merriment.

Once upon a time some fishermen who were crossing the " Sea-stream of the Blue Men " in calm weather found one of the blue fellows sleeping on the surface. They seized him, and, lifting him into the boat, bound him tightly with a rope. He slept so soundly that although the fishermen let him fall out of their hands he did not awake.

They resolved to take him to the shore, but they had not gone far when two Blue Men bobbed above the clear waters and shouted:—

> Duncan will be one, Donald will be two,
>   Will you need another ere you reach the shore?

The skipper of the boat was about to shout two lines in reply, but, before he could speak, the Blue Man in the boat opened his eyes, and with a quick movement he snapped the rope that bound him as easily as if it had been only an oat straw, and answered:—

> Duncan's voice I hear, Donald too is near,
>   But no need of helpers has strong Ian More.

As he spoke he leapt out of the boat into the sea. That was how the fishermen came to know that all the Blue Men have names of their own.

The Green Ladies are different from the fairies, who are called " Wee Folk ", for, like the Blue Men, they are of human size. Some of them are withered old hags, resembling Beira in the winter season, and some of them are as fair as Beira in her summer girlhood. They have power to change their forms at will. A Green Lady may sometimes deceive a traveller by appearing before him in the form of his lady-love, and, after speaking to him for a time, turn away with mocking laughter and vanish from sight. Perhaps, too, she may appear as a dog, and torment shepherds by driving their sheep hither and thither in wild confusion.

Each Green Lady lives alone in a solitary place, either below a river or waterfall or in a green knoll, a forest, or a deep ravine. One is rarely seen in daytime. The Green Lady wanders about in the dusk of late evening, in moonlight, or in darkness. She is ever a deceiver, and woe to the traveller who has not the knowledge how to overcome her spells, for she may drown him at a river ford or lead him over the edge of a precipice. It is difficult to fight against her, for if she asks a man what weapon he has, and he names it, she can, by working magic, make the weapon quite harmless.

One evening a smith was riding homeward from battle on his horse, and when it was growing dusk he reached a ford. Suddenly a Green Lady rose out of the water in front of him.

"Stop!" she cried; "you cannot ride across."

Said the man: "Begone! O evil one, or I shall smite you."

"What have you to fight with?" she asked.

Said the man: "I have my sword."

Immediately he named his sword it lost its power to do her injury.

The Green Lady laughed mockingly, and then asked: "What else have you to fight with?"

Said the man: "I have my spear."

When he named the spear it became as useless as the sword.

The Green Lady laughed again, a shrill mocking laugh. "Have you room for a rider behind you?" she asked.

Said the man: "Yes, and there is room also for a rider in front."

As he spoke he seized the Green Lady, lifted her up in front of him, threw the reins over her head, and said: "Now I have you in my power."

"You will never leave the ford," she answered, "because your sword and spear have been made useless to you."

Said the man: "I have still one weapon left."

"Which one is that?" she asked.

Said the smith: "The sharp bright weapon against my leg."

He meant the dirk in his right stocking, but as he did not mention its name, the Green Lady could not make it useless.

"Then I will leave you," cried the lady in alarm.

Said the smith: "You cannot leave me until I choose to let you go. The reins are about you, and you cannot move beyond them, for the magic power has now been taken from you and has passed to me."

The Green Lady knew well that this was so. She knew also that she would have to do whatever the man ordered her to do before he would set her free.

The horse was urged forward by the smith, and the ford was crossed in safety. Then the animal trotted across the moor as the moon rose over the hills, shining fair and bright.

"Let me go," the Green Lady cried, "and I shall give you a herd of speckled cattle."

Said the man: "You will have to give me a herd of cattle, but still I shall not let you go."

The horse went on, and the Green Lady wept tears of sorrow and anger.

"Let me go," she cried, "and I shall build for you to-night a house which fire will not burn nor water or storm wind injure, and it shall be charmed against all evil beings."

The man reined up his horse, and said: "Fulfil your promise, and I shall set you free."

He dismounted, and the Green Lady dismounted also. The smith tied the reins round her, and repeated his command.

"Your wish will be fulfilled," she said.

Then the Green Lady uttered a loud cry, which was heard over seven hills. The cry was repeated over and over again by Big Angus of the Rock (Echo), a lonely spirit who is at everyone's service. Big Angus is a son of Beira, and it is told he was wont to cause his mother much trouble by contradicting her orders and giving orders of his own, for he desired to be King of the Universe, although he was weak-minded and light-headed. To punish him, Beira shut him inside a rock, and compelled him ever after to repeat any words that were said in his hearing. Ever since that day Big Angus has had to repeat over and over again everything he hears in his lonely rocky prison.

So Big Angus repeated the cry of the Green Lady, which was a command to fairies and goblins to come to her aid. As these little people fear all Green Ladies, they answered her cry without delay. They came from the hill-tops and from inside cliffs, from green knolls in lonely moors and deep forests, and from every other haunt they loved. Those that were dancing ceased to dance, and those that were setting out on journeys turned back. They crossed the moors jumping like crickets, and came through the air like birds and gathered round the Green Lady, waiting to obey her.

She set them to work at once to hew wood and gather stones. They cut down trees in the Rowan

Wood, and quarried stones below a waterfall. As they went on working, the Green Lady cried out:—

> Two stones over one stone,
> One stone over two stones—
>   Work speedily, work speedily—
> Bring every timber from the wood
>   But mulberry, but mulberry.

The house was built very quickly.   Across the moor the fairies stood in two rows—one row from the house to the waterfall and one from the house to the Rowan Wood.   The stones that were quarried were passed along from hand to hand, and so were the pieces of timber that were hewed down and sawed and dressed.

When the dawn was beginning to appear in the eastern sky the house was ready, and all the fairies and goblins vanished from sight.

"Set me free," cried the Green Lady.

The smith said: "I shall set you free when you have promised not to do me any injury."

"I promise that readily," said she.

Said the smith: "Promise also that neither I nor my children will ever be drowned by you in the fords of the three rivers."

He named the rivers he referred to.   They all flowed near his home.

The Green Lady promised that also.   Then the smith set her free, and she cried: "You have not named the fourth river. Let you and your children beware!"

As she spoke she went past the smith like a green flame. He never again saw her, but seven years afterwards one of his sons was drowned in the ford of the fourth river he had not named, and then he knew that the Green Lady had taken her revenge.

Other Green Ladies have made friends with certain families, and have kept watch over their houses, shielding them from harm. Once a poor fisherman lost his boat, and sat down on the beach at a river mouth lamenting his fate. A Green Lady appeared before him, and said: "If I give you a new boat will you divide your fish with me?"

Said the fisherman: "I promise to do so."

Next morning he found a new boat lying on the beach. He went out to sea and caught many fish. When he returned to the shore he left half of his catch on a green knoll on the river bank. The Green Lady was well pleased, and helped the man to prosper.

One evening, however, he left no fish for her. He went out to sea next day as usual, but did not catch anything. Sad was his heart when he returned home empty-handed, but it was even sadder next morning when he found that his boat had been smashed to pieces during the night in a storm which had risen suddenly and raged until daybreak. He never again saw the Green Lady, and he had reason to be sorry that he had not kept his bargain with her.

There was once a Green Lady who received favours from a bold pirate whose name was Mac Ean Yeer. She kept watch over him on sea and land, so that he was always able to escape from those who pursued him. The Green Lady advised him to paint one side of his boat black and the other side white, so that watchers on the shore would see a black boat passing to the north and a white boat passing to the south, and thus be deceived, thinking the boat which went out to attack a galley was not the same one as they saw returning. In time, when the people came to know the trick, they said of deceitful persons:

> He's black on one side and white on the other,
> Like the boat of Mac Ean Yeer.

Mac Ean lived to be an old man, and when he died in Islay the Green Lady shrieked aloud and passed northward. The shriek was heard in Mull, and ere the echoes died away she had reached the Coolin Hills in Skye.

CHAPTER VI

Conall and the Thunder Hag

Among the hags who served Beira was the Thunder Hag. When Angus began to reign she fled across the ocean to a lonely island, where she plotted to wreak vengeance by bringing disaster to man and beast, because they had rejoiced when Beira was overcome.

One day in midsummer, when all the land was bathed in warm, bright sunshine and the sea was lulled to sleep, the Thunder Hag came over Scotland in a black chariot drawn by fierce red hounds and surrounded by heavy clouds. The sky was darkened, and as the hag drew near, the rattling of the chariot wheels and the baying of the hounds sounded loud and fearsome. She rode from sea to sea, over hill and moor, and threw fireballs at the deep forests, which set them ablaze. Terror spread through the land as the chariot passed in smoke and clouds.

On the next day the hag came back. She threw more fireballs on forests of fir and silver birch, and they burned fiercely.   Dry heather on the moors and the sun-dried grass were also swept by flame.

The king was greatly troubled, and he sent forth his chief warriors to slay the hag; but they fled in terror when they saw her coming near.

On the third day she returned.   Then the king called for Conall Curlew, the fearless hero, and spoke to him, saying: "My kingdom will be destroyed if the hag is not slain.   I need your help, O brave and noble one."

Said Conall: "I shall go out against the hag, O king, and if I do not slay her to-day, I may slay her on the morrow."

Conall went forth, and when he saw and heard the chariot drawing near he went up to the summit of a high mountain and waited to attack her.   But the hag kept herself hidden behind a cloud which surrounded the chariot.   Conall had to return to the king without having done anything.

"I could not see the hag because of the dark cloud," he said.

"If she comes again to-morrow," the king said, "you may fare better."

Conall then made preparations for the next coming of the hag.   He went out into the fields that were nigh to the royal castle, and separated all the lambs from the sheep, all the calves from the cows, and all the foals from the mares.   When morning came on there was great tumult among the animals.

There never was heard before such a bleating of sheep, such a lowing of cattle, or neighing of mares, in the land of Alba, and it was piteous to hear the cries of the lambs, and the calves, and the foals which were taken from their mothers. The men were filled with wonder at the thing Conall had done, nor could they understand why he had done it, and the hearts of the women were touched by the cries of the young animals, and they wept to hear them.

It was indeed a morning of sorrow and wailing when the cloud in which the hag's chariot was hidden came nigh to the castle. The cloud darkened the heavens, and when it passed over the wooded hill the fire-balls set the trees in flame, and all the people fled before the cloud and concealed themselves in caves and in holes in the ground, all except the warriors, who waited, trembling, with deep eyes and pale faces.

Conall stood alone on a green knoll, and his spear was in his hand.

When the cloud came over the valley of the castle, the hag heard the cries of the animals that assailed her ears, and so great was her curiosity that she peered over the edge of the black cloud.

Great fear fell on the hearts of the warriors

when they saw the horrible face of the hoary-headed hag; but Conall was a man without fear, and he was waiting for the hag to reveal herself.

As soon as he saw her, he swung his right arm over his shoulder, and he cast the spear towards the cloud. The swallow does not dart swifter than the spear of Conall darted through the air.

The hag was wounded, and threw wide her grisly paws and sank down within the chariot. She called to the black hounds: "Race quickly!" and they ran swiftly towards the west. The sound of the rattling of the chariot wheels grew fainter and fainter as it passed out of sight.

The clouds which the hag passed over swiftly in her flight were rent in twain, and rain fell in torrents, quenching the fires that were in the woods and on the moors.

There was great rejoicing in the land because of the mighty deed done by Conall, and the king honoured that noble hero by placing a gold ring on his finger, a gold armlet on his arm, and a gold necklet on his neck.

There was peace and prosperity in the land after that. The hag did not return again, so greatly did she dread Conall Curlew, the hero of heroes.

CHAPTER VII

Story of Finlay and the Giants

Finlay the hunter lived with his sister in a lonely little house among the mountains, and near at hand there were giants who were descendants of Beira. This giant clan was ruled over by a hag-queen who was very old and fierce and cunning. She had great stores of silver and gold in her cave, and also a gold-hilted magic sword and a magic wand. When she struck a stone pillar with this wand it became a warrior, and if she put the gold-hilted sword into his hand, the greatest and strongest hero in the world would be unable to combat against him with success.

Every day that Finlay went out to hunt he warned his sister, saying: "Do not open the windows on the north side of the house, or let the fire go out."

His sister did not, however, heed his warning always. One day she shut the windows on the south side of the house, and opened those on the north side, and allowed the fire to go out.

She wondered what would happen, and she

had not long to wait, for a young giant came towards the house and entered it. He had assumed a comely form, and spoke pleasantly to Finlay's sister. They became very friendly, and the giant made the foolish girl promise not to tell her brother of his visits. After that the girl began to quarrel with Finlay. This went on for a time.

One day when Finlay was returning to his home he saw a little shieling in a place where no shieling used to be. He wondered who dwelt in it, and walked towards the door and entered. He saw an old woman sitting on the floor, and she bade him welcome.

"Sit down," she said. "Your name is Finlay."

"That is true," answered he; "who are you and whence come you?"

"I am called Wise Woman," she answered. "I have come here to protect and guide you. Alas! you do not know that you are in danger of your life. A young giant has bewitched your sister, and is waiting to kill you this very day with a sharp blue sword."

"Alas!" cried Finlay, who sorrowed to think of his sister.

Being forewarned, the hunter was prepared. When he returned home he set his fierce dogs on the giant, and threw a pot of boiling water over him. The giant fled shrieking towards his cave, and Finlay's sister followed him.

Then the hunter was left alone in the house. His heart shook with terror because he feared that one of the older giants would come against him to avenge the injury done to the young giant.

He had good reason to be afraid. As soon as the young giant reached the cave, his brother cried: " I shall go forth and deal with the hunter."

" I had better go myself," his father said fiercely.

" It is I who should go," growled the fierce grey hag.

" I spoke first," urged the young giant's brother, and sprang towards the mouth of the cave in the gathering dusk.

Finlay waited alone in his little house. The door was shut and securely barred, and the peat fire glowed bright and warm, yet he shivered with the coldness of terror. He listened long and anxiously, and at length heard a growing noise like distant thunder. Stones rumbled down the hillside as the giant raced on, and when he entered a bog the mud splashed heavily against the cliffs. Finlay knew then that a giant was coming, and ere long he heard his voice roaring outside the door: "Fith! foth! foogie! The door is shut against a stranger. Open and let me in." He did not wait for Finlay to answer, but burst the door open with a blow. The hunter stood behind the fire which burned in the middle of the room, his bow in his hand and an arrow ready. He fired as the giant entered, but did not kill him. The giant shrieked and leapt towards Finlay, but the dogs made fierce attack. Then the hunter shot another arrow from his bow and killed the giant.

Next morning Finlay hastened to the shieling of Wise Woman, taking with him the giant's head.

"Well, valiant lad," she exclaimed, "how fared it with you last night?"

Finlay told her all that had taken place, and explained that it was owing to the help given him by the dogs he was able to slay the giant.

"There is need of the dogs," Wise Woman said, "but the day of their great need has yet to come."

That evening Finlay again sat alone in his house, wondering what would happen next. No sooner did night come on than he heard a noise like distant thunder, but much louder than on the night before. Great boulders rumbled down the hill-side, and mud splashed on the cliffs. Another and more terrible giant was coming, seeking to be avenged.

"Thoth! Thoth! Foogie!" roared his heavy voice outside the house. "I smell a man inside. Open the door that I may enter. Although you killed my son last night, you shall not slay me."

He burst the door open, and as he did so the house shook. Finlay feared the roof was about to fall upon him, but he feared more when he beheld the giant in the firelight, for the monster had five heads.

He drew his bow and shot an arrow. The giant paused. Finlay shot a second arrow, which, like the first, wounded the monster, but did not kill him. Then the hunter drew his sword and smote him heavily, but his wounds were not mortal. The giant stretched out his grisly hands to seize Finlay, but the dogs leapt at him, and a fierce struggle took place, but in the end Finlay triumphed, and the giant was slain.

Next morning the hunter went to the shieling of Wise Woman, and told her of the night of terror and the long and deadly combat. "The dogs," he said, "helped me. But for the dogs I should have been overcome."

Said Wise Woman: "There is need for the dogs, but the day of their greatest need has yet to come. To-night the fierce grey hag will seek to avenge the death of her husband and son. Beware of her, O valiant lad! She will not come raging and roaring like the giants, but gently and mannerly. She will call to you in a meek and mild voice, asking you to let her in. But, remember, it is her intention to take your life. Do as I instruct you and all will be well."

Wise Woman then gave him instructions, and he went home. When night came on there was silence all around.   Finlay waited alone, listening intently, and the silence terrified him more than the noises like distant thunder he had heard on the two previous nights.   He shook and shivered beside the warm bright peat fire, waiting and waiting and listening.   At length he sprang up suddenly, for he heard a rustling sound like the wind stirring dead leaves.   A moment later a weak patient voice outside the door called: "I am old and weary.   I have need of food and of shelter for the night.   Open and let me in."

Finlay went to the door and made answer: "I shall let you in, old woman, if you promise to be civil and mannerly, and not do me an injury."

Said the hag: "Oh! I shall give no trouble. I promise to be civil and mannerly.   Let me enter your house."

Finlay opened the door, and the hag walked in. She looked a poor frail old woman, and seemed to be very weary.   When she had curtsied to Finlay, she sat down on one side of the fire. Finlay sat down on the opposite side.

The hag stretched out her hands to warm them, and began to look about her.   Finlay's three dogs were prowling up and down the room, snarling angrily and showing their teeth.

"These are fierce dogs," the widow said. "Arise and tie them with thongs."

" The dogs will not do any harm to a peaceable old woman," said Finlay.

"Tie them up in any case, I pray you. I dislike angry dogs."

" I cannot do that, old woman, because I have nothing to tie them with."

Said the hag: " I will give you three red ribbons from my cap. They are strong enough to hold a big ship at anchor."

Finlay took the red ribbons from her and pretended to tie up the dogs. But he only made them lie down in a corner.

" Have you tied up the dogs?" asked the hag very softly.

"You can see for yourself that they are lying now with their necks close together," Finlay answered. The hag looked at the dogs, and believing they had been secured with her magic ribbons, smiled to herself.

She sat beside the fire in silence for a time, and Finlay sat opposite her. After a time the hunter noticed that she was growing bigger and bigger.

"What means this?" cried Findlay. "You seem to be growing bigger and bigger."

"Oh, no, my darling!" she answered. " The cold of the night made me shrink, and now I am feeling more comfortable beside your warm bright fire."

There was silence again, and Finlay watched

her for a time and then cried: "You are growing bigger, without doubt. You may be pleased or displeased because I say so, but you cannot deny it."

The hag frowned and answered angrily: "I am growing bigger, as you say. What of that? You fear me now, and you have good reason to. You slew my husband last night, and you slew my son on the night before. I shall certainly kill you to-night."

When she had spoken thus she sprang to her feet in full height, and the house shook about her and above. Finlay sprang to his feet also, and as he did so the hag seized him by the hair of his head. Having promised not to injure him inside the house—a promise she could not break— she dragged him outside. The three dogs rose, and sprang through the door after her.

Finlay wrestled fiercely with the hag, and the two twisted and turned hither and thither. The mother of the young giant would have killed him without delay, but the dogs kept attacking her, and gave her much trouble. At length, with the help of the dogs, Finlay managed to throw her down. She lay upon one of her arms, and the dogs held the other.

"Oh! let me rise to my feet," cried the hag, who had no power to struggle when she lay on the ground.

Said Finlay: "I shall not allow you to rise up."

"Allow me to ransom myself," the hag pleaded.

Said Finlay: "What ransom will you give?"

"I have a trunk of gold and a trunk of silver in my cave. You shall get both," she answered.

Said Finlay: "Having overcome you, these are mine already."

"I will give you a gold-hilted sword which is in my cave," the hag then promised. "He who wields this magic sword will overcome any man or any beast in the world."

Said Finlay: "The sword is mine already."

"I will give you a magic rod if you spare me," the hag cried then. "It is a matchless weapon. It can also work wonders. If you strike a stone pillar with it, the pillar will turn into a warrior, and if you will put the gold-hilted sword in this warrior's hand, he will conquer the world for you."

Said Finlay: "Your wand is mine already by right of conquest. What else have you to offer for ransom?"

"Alas!" the hag cried, "I have naught else to give you."

Said Finlay: "Then you shall die. The world will be well rid of you."

He slew the fierce hag, and then arose quickly and put "red moss" (sphagnum moss) on his wounds and sores, so that they might be healed speedily. Next morning he arose and went and informed Wise Woman of what had taken place, saying: "It was chiefly owing to the dogs that the hag was overcome."

Said Wise Woman: "O valiant hero! the dogs have now had their day."

Then Finlay told about the treasure in the cave, and said: "I know not how I can obtain the gold and silver, the gold-hilted sword, and the magic wand."

Said Wise Woman: "To-night my daughter and I will go with you to the giants' cave. I will take my own magic wand with me."

When darkness came on the three went to the cave. They set to work and gathered armfuls of dry heather, which they heaped up at the cave mouth and set on fire, so that the young giant within might be choked by the fumes and scorched by the flames. Soon the giant crawled to the mouth of the cave, panting heavily. He came through the smoke dazed and half blinded. Suddenly a warning light appeared on his forehead.

Finlay drew his bow and said: "I will shoot."

"Do not shoot," Wise Woman warned him. "A wound would only make him fiercer, and the dogs would be of no use to you among the fire. If he is allowed to escape out of the flare, the dogs would not see him in the darkness. I shall strike him with my magic wand. I can strike once only, and if I fail he will strike the next blow with the gold-hilted sword which is in his hand."

The giant scattered the fire to get out of the cave, but ere he could rise Wise Woman smote him on the head with her magic wand, and he fell down dead.

When they entered the cave they found that Finlay's sister was within. But she was dead; she had perished in her cave prison.

Finlay took out all the treasure that was in the cave, and carried it to the shieling of Wise Woman. Then he tested the magic wand. He struck a stone pillar with it, and the pillar became a warrior. Then he struck the warrior, and he became a stone pillar again.

"This is wonderful," Finlay exclaimed.

"It is indeed," said Wise Woman. Then she told him that he must visit the king next day and inform him of all that had taken place, and she made him take a vow not to enter the palace.

Next day Finlay set out to the palace of the king. When he reached it he bade the royal servants inform the king that the great giants had been slain.

Said the king: "Let the valiant hero come within."

Finlay, however, declined to enter the palace, and sent him word, saying: "I dare not enter your palace, as I have a vow to fulfil."

The king came outside and spoke to Finlay, saying: "Come within. I shall give you my daughter, the princess, in marriage. You shall also have half of my kingdom as long as I live, and the remainder shall be yours when I die."

Said Finlay: "I give you thanks, O king, but I cannot enter."

When he had spoken thus, he walked towards a grey stone pillar and smote it with the magic wand. The pillar became a noble warrior. Then he smote the warrior, and he became a pillar again. The king was greatly astonished, and exclaimed: "I have never seen anything like this before."

He went into the palace to give orders about Finlay, whom he wished to detain, but when he came out again he found that the hunter had gone.

The king sent out foot-runners and horsemen to make search throughout the kingdom for Finlay, but they returned without having seen aught of him.

Finlay married the daughter of Wise Woman, and he prospered. Years went past. Finlay had a family of three sons. He loved the boys very dearly, and spent happy days roaming with them among the mountains. All went well with him until Wise Woman died. Then misfortune overtook him. His wife died, and all his wealth was stolen from him by night robbers who were in league with the giants. He lost also the magic wand, but he kept possession of the gold-hilted sword. Nor did his troubles have end when he became poor again, for a witch cast spells on his three young sons and smote them with a magic wand. Then the boys were transformed into three beautiful white dogs and fled away.

Finlay was stricken with sorrow, and set out to search for his children. He crossed mountains and moors, following in the tracks of the three white dogs, but without avail. The day went past and evening came on, and still he hastened onward. When darkness had fallen he came to a small glen and saw a light. He walked towards the light, and found it shone from the window of a house. At this house he asked for a night's lodgings, and it was given to him. The old man of the house spoke to him, saying: "You are sad and tearful, O stranger. Are you searching for your three sons?"

Said Finlay: "Oh, yes! Have you seen them?"

" They are travelling over mountain and moor," said the old man. " I cannot do anything to help you. To-morrow night you will reach the house of a brother of mine, and if he will not help you, I do not know what you should do."

Finlay resumed his journey next day, and when darkness came on he reached the house of the old man's brother, who said: "Your sons are travelling over mountain and moor as three white dogs. They cannot rest or stay, for they must travel by day and by night. I cannot do anything for you. To-morrow night you will reach the house of my elder brother, and he will give you advice."

Next night Finlay reached the house of the elder brother, and he said: "Your sons will remain under spells until Doomsday if you will not do one thing."

"What is that?" Finlay asked.

"You must have three garments made of bog-cotton, and leave them on a hill which your sons in dog form are now running round. When they see the white garments they will put them on. Each one of the garments will take you a year to make, unless you get a band of women to collect the bog-cotton, and a band of women to spin and weave."

"Alas!" Finlay exclaimed, "I cannot hire workers, because I have lost all I possessed."

"You still have the gold-hilted sword," the man said. "It may be of service to you."

Next morning Finlay resumed his journey with a heavy heart indeed. He went on until dusk. Then he heard cries of sorrow and despair. In another moment he beheld a great giant coming towards him, dragging a young man whom he had taken captive. Finlay drew his gold-hilted

sword, and spoke boldly to the giant, saying:
"Let your captive go free, or I shall smite you."

"Ho, ho!" laughed the giant. "Your sword
will bend like a grass blade when it strikes my
body."

As he spoke he stretched out his right hand
to seize Finlay and take him captive also. But
Finlay smote the giant with the gold-hilted magic
sword, and slew him.

The young man was overjoyed and thanked
Finlay, praising him for his valour. "Come with
me to my father's house," he said. "He is the
king of this country, and will reward you."

The young prince had many sores and wounds,
and Finlay put "red moss" (sphagnum) on them.
Then the two went together to the palace and
entered it. When the king heard his son's story,
he said to Finlay: "You shall stay here, O
wanderer, and I shall make you rich and pros-
perous."

"Alas!" Finlay exclaimed. "I cannot tarry
here except for one night."

The queen came forward and said: "You are
sad and unhappy, O stranger! What is the cause
of your grief?"

Finlay told the queen about his lost sons and
his weary and fruitless search for them.

Said the queen: "One of the king's shepherds
has told me that every morning when he goes out

he sees three beautiful white dogs on the green
hill nigh to the palace."

"Ah! these are my sons," Finlay cried. Then
he told the queen what the elder of the three old
men had said.

The queen listened intently, and then spoke,
saying: "I shall give you mine aid. Until I
have had made the garments of bog-cotton, there
will be no rest for me, O stranger, because you
have rescued my son from death."

Next morning the queen sent women to collect bog-cotton and women to spin and weave.
The bog-cotton was collected speedily, for hundreds of women went out to obey the queen's
command. Then the yarn was spun; it was put
into the weaver's loom and woven. Then women
sewed the garments, which were afterwards washed
and bleached until they were as white and soft as
new-fallen snow on a mountain top. The garments were laid on the green hill when the sun
was setting.

Next morning Finlay went out early to look
for his sons, and the prince whom he had rescued
went with him. They found that the white garments had been taken away, but the boys could
not be seen anywhere. Finlay and the prince
searched far and wide for them in vain, and then
returned to the palace.

A week went past, and, Finlay sorrowed greatly.

Each morning he asked the shepherd if he had seen either the boys or the white dogs, and the shepherd answered saying: "No, I have not seen the white dogs on the green hill."

On the seventh day three youths appeared at the door of the palace and asked to see the stranger who resided there. Finlay came towards them with tears falling from his eyes.

"What ails you?" one of the youths asked.

Said Finlay: "I am mourning for my three beloved sons whom I shall never behold again."

"We are your sons, O father!" the youths exclaimed together.

Finlay dried his tears which blinded him, and then recognized his lost sons. He embraced them and kissed them, and took them before the king and the queen, who bade them welcome.

After that Finlay dwelt in the palace of the king, and his three sons grew up and became mighty warriors.

CHAPTER VIII

Heroes on the Green Isle

There was once a prince who found himself in the Green Isle of the West, and this is how the story of his adventures are told:—

The Prince of the Kingdom of Level-Plains set out on his travels to see the world, and he went northward and westward until he came to a red glen surrounded by mountains. There he met with a proud hero, who spoke to him, saying: "Whence come you, and whither are you going?"

Said the prince: "I am searching for my equal," and as he spoke he drew his sword. He was a bold and foolish young man.

"I have no desire to fight with you," the proud hero answered. "Go your way in peace."

The prince was jealous of the hero who spoke thus so calmly and proudly, and said: "Draw your sword or die."

Then he darted forward. The hero swerved aside to escape the sword-thrust, and next moment he leapt upon the prince, whom he overcame after a brief struggle, and bound with a rope. Then he carried him to the top of a cliff, and said: "You are not fit to be among men. Go and dwell among the birds of prey."

He flung him over the cliff. The prince fell heavily into a large nest on a ledge of rock, the nest of the queen of eagles—a giant bird of great strength.

For a time he lay stunned by his fall. When he came to himself he regretted his folly, and said: "If ever I escape from this place I shall behave wisely, and challenge no man without cause."

He found himself in the great nest with three young eagles in it. The birds were hungry, and when the prince held his wrists towards one, it pecked the rope that bound them until it was severed; so then he stretched his legs towards another bird, and it severed the rope about his ankles. He was thus set free. He rose up and looked about him. The ledge jutted out in mid-air on the cliff-side, and the prince saw it was impossible either to ascend or descend the slippery rocks. Behind the nest there was a deep cave, into which he crept. There he crouched, waiting to see what would happen next.

The young birds shrieked with hunger, and the prince was hungry also. Ere long the queen of eagles came to the nest. Her great body and

outstretched wings cast a shadow like that of a
thunder cloud, and when she perched on the ledge
of rock, it shook under her weight.

The eagle brought a hare for her young and
laid it in the nest. Then she flew away. The
prince at once crept out of the cave and seized
the hare. He gathered together a bundle of dry
twigs from the side of the nest and kindled a fire
in the cave, and cooked the hare and ate it. The
smoke from the fire smothered the young birds,
and when the queen of eagles returned she found
that they were dead. She knew at once that an
enemy must be near at hand, and looked into
the cave. There she saw the prince, who at
once drew his sword bravely and fought long and
fiercely against her, inflicting many wounds to
defend himself. But he was no good match for
that fierce bird, and at length she seized him in
her talons and, springing off the ledge of rock,
flew through the air with him. His body was
soon torn by the eagle's claws and sore with
wounds. The eagle, also sorely wounded, rose
up among the clouds, and turning westward flew
hurriedly over the sea. Her shadow blotted out
the sunshine on the waters as she passed in her
flight, and boatmen lowered their sails, thinking
that a sudden gust of wind was sweeping down
upon them.

The prince swooned, and regained conscious-

ness, and swooned again. As the bird flew on-
wards the sun scorched him. Then she dropped
him into the sea, and he found the waters cold as
ice. "Alas!" he thought, "I shall be drowned."
He rose to the surface and began to swim towards
an island near at hand, but the eagle pounced down,
and seizing him again, rose high in the air. Once
again she dropped him, and then he swooned and
remembered no more, until he found himself lying
on a green bank on a pleasant shore. The sun
was shining, birds sang sweetly among blossoming
trees of great beauty, and the sea-waves made
music on the beach. Somewhere near he could
hear a river fairy singing a summer song.

Next he heard behind him a splashing of water,
and a shower of pearly drops fell upon his right
arm as he lay there weak and helpless. But
no sooner did the water touch his arm than it
became strong again. The splashing continued,
and he twisted himself this way and that until
the pearly spray had drenched every part of his
body. Then he felt strong and active again, and
sprang to his feet. He looked round, and saw
that the showers of spray had come from a well
in which the wounded queen of eagles was bathing herself. The prince knew then that this was
a Well of Healing.

He remembered how fiercely the eagle had
dealt with him, and wished he still had his sword.

Having no sword, he drew his dirk and crept softly towards the well. He waited a moment, crouching behind a bush, and then, raising his dirk, struck off the eagle's head. But he found it was not easy to kill the monster in the Well of Healing. No sooner was the head struck off than it sprang on again. Thrice he beheaded the eagle, and thrice the head was restored. When, however, he struck off the head a fourth time, he held the blade of his dirk between the head and neck until the eagle was dead. Then he dragged the body out of the well, and buried the head in the ground. Having done so, he bathed in the well, and when he came out of it, all his wounds were healed, and he found himself as active and able as if he had just awakened from a long sleep.

He looked about him, and saw fruit growing on a blossoming tree. He wondered at that, but being very hungry he plucked the fruit and ate it. Never before had he tasted fruit of such sweet flavour. Feeling refreshed, and at the same time happy and contented, he turned to walk through the forest of beautiful trees and singing birds, when he saw three men coming towards him. He spoke to them, saying: "Who are you, and whence come you?" They answered: "There is no time to tell. If you are not a dweller on this island, come with us while there is yet time to escape."

The prince wondered to hear them speak thus, but, having learned wisdom, he followed them in silence. They went down the beach and entered a boat. The prince stepped in also. Two of the men laid oars in the rowlocks, and one sat at the stern to steer. In another moment the boat darted forward, cleaving the waves; but not until it had gone half a league did the man at the helm speak to the prince. He said simply: "Look behind and tell me what you see."

The prince looked, and all he saw was a green speck on the horizon. A cry of wonder escaped his lips.

"The speck you see," said the steersman, "is the Green Isle. It is now floating westward to the edge of the ocean."

Then the prince understood why the men had hurried to escape, and he realized that if he had not taken their advice, he would have been carried away beyond the reach of human aid.

Said the steersman: "Now we can speak. Who are you, and whence come you?"

The prince told the story of his adventure with the queen of eagles, and the men in the boat listened intently. When he was done, the steersman said: "Now listen, and hear what we have gone through."

This was the story told by the steersman, whose

name was Conall Curlew, the names of the rowers being Garna and Cooimer.

Yesterday at dawn we beheld the Green Isle lying no farther distant from the shore than a league. The fourth man who was with us is named Mac-a-moir, and he spoke, saying: "Let us visit the Green Isle and explore it. I am told that the king has a daughter named Sunbeam, who is of peerless beauty, and that he will give her as a bride to the bravest hero who visits his castle. He who is bold enough will come with me."

We all went down to the beach with Mac-a-moir, and launched a boat to cross over to the Green Island. The tide favoured us, and we soon reached it. We moored the boat in a sheltered creek, and landed. The beauties of the forest tempted us to linger, and eat fruit and listen to the melodious songs of numerous birds, but Mac-a-moir pressed us to hasten on. Soon we came to a green valley in which there was a castle. I, Conall, knocked at the gate, and a sentinel asked what I sought, and I answered: "I have come to ask for Sunbeam, daughter of the King of Green Isle, to be the bride of Mac-a-moir."

Word was sent to the king, who said: "He who seeks my daughter Sunbeam must first hold combat with my warriors."

"I am ready for combat," Mac-a-moir declared.

The gate was opened, and the heroes entered. Mac-a-moir drew his sword, and the first warrior came against him. Ere long Mac-a-moir struck him down. A second warrior, and then a third, fought and fell also in turn.

Said the king, when the third warrior fell: "You have overcome the champion of Green Isle."

"Bring forth the next best," Mac-a-moir called.

Said the king: "I fear, my hero, that you wish to slay all my warriors one by one. You have proved your worth. Now let us test you in another manner. My daughter dwells in a high tower on the summit of a steep hill. He who can take her out will have her for his bride. He will also receive two-thirds of my kingdom while I live, and the whole of my kingdom when I die."

All who were present then went towards the tower, which stood on three high pillars.

"Who will try first to take out the king's daughter?" I asked.

Said Mac-a-moir: "I shall try first."

He tried, but he failed. He could neither climb the pillars nor throw them down.

Said the king: "Many a man has tried to take my daughter out of this tower, but each one has failed to do so. You had better all return home."

The other two, Garna and Cooimer, made attempts to shake down the tower, but without success.

Said the king: "It is no use trying. My daughter cannot be taken out."

Then I, Conall, stepped forward. I seized one of the pillars and shook it until it broke. The tower toppled over, and as it came down I grasped the Princess Sunbeam in my arms, and placed her standing beside me.

"Your daughter is now won," I called to the king.

The Princess Sunbeam smiled sweetly, and the king said: "Yes, indeed, she has been won."

"I have won her," I, Conall, reminded him, "for Mac-a-moir."

Said the king: "He who will marry Sunbeam must remain on Green Isle."

"So be it," Mac-a-moir answered him as he took Sunbeam's hand in his and walked towards the castle, following the king.

A great feast was held in the castle, and Mac-a-moir and the princess were married.

Said the king: "I am well pleased with Mac-a-moir. It is my desire that his three companions should remain with him and be my warriors."

I, Conall, told him: "It is our desire to return to our own country."

The king did not answer. He sat gloomily at

the board, and when the wedding feast was ended he walked from the feasting hall.

Mac-a-moir came and spoke to us soon afterwards, saying: "If it is your desire to go away, make haste and do so now, for the king is about to move Green Isle far westward towards the realms of the setting sun."

We bade him farewell, and took our departure. You met us as we hastened towards the boat, and it is as well that you came with us.

The prince dwelt a time with Conall and his companions. Then he returned to his own land, and related all that had taken place to his father, the King of Level-Plains.

CHAPTER IX

A Vision of the Dead

There once dwelt in Nithsdale a woman who was enabled by fairy aid to see the spirits of the dead in the Other World. This was how it came about. One day she sat spinning wool in her house. Her baby lay in a cradle beside her, listening to the soft humming sound of the spinning wheel and her mother's sweet song. Suddenly a rustling, like the rustling of dead leaves in the wind, was heard at the door. The woman looked up and saw a beautiful lady, clad in green and carrying a baby. She entered, and smiling sweetly, spoke and said: "Will you nurse my bonnie baby until I return?"

The woman answered: "Yes, I shall do that."

She took the baby in her arms, and the lady went away, promising to return. But the day went past and night came on, and still she did not come back for her child. The woman wondered greatly, but she wondered even more next morning when she awoke to find beside her bed beautiful new clothes for her children, and some delicious cakes. Being very poor she was glad to dress her children in the new clothes, and to find that they fitted well. The cakes were of wheaten bread and had a honey flavour. It was a great delight to the children to eat them.

The lady did not return that day or the next day. Weeks went past, and the woman nursed the strange child. Months went past, and still the lady stayed away. On many a morning wheaten cakes with honey flavour were found in the house, and when the children's clothes were nearly worn out, new clothing was provided for them as mysteriously as before.

Summer came on, and one evening the lady, clad in green, again entered the house. A child who was playing on the floor stretched forth her hands to grasp the shining silver spangles that adorned her gown, but, to his surprise, his hands passed through them as if they were sunbeams. The woman perceived this, and knew that her visitor was a fairy.

Said the fairy lady: "You have been kind to my bonnie baby; I will now take her away."

The woman was sorry to part with the child, and said: "You have a right to her, but I love her dearly."

Said the fairy: "Come with me, and I shall show you my house."

The woman went outside with the fairy. They

walked through a wood together, and then began
to climb a green hill on the sunny side. When
they were half-way to the top, the fairy said
something which the woman did not understand.
No sooner had she spoken than the turf on a
bank in front of them lifted up and revealed a
door. This door opened, and the two entered
through the doorway. When they did so, the
turf came down and the door was shut.

The woman found herself in a bare chamber
which was dimly lighted.

"Now you shall see my home," said the fairy
woman, who took from her waist-belt a goblet
containing a green liquid. She dropped three
drops of this liquid in the woman's left eye, and
said: "Look now."

The woman looked, and was filled with wonder.
A beautiful country stretched out in front of her.
There were green hills fringed by trees, crystal
streams flashing in sunshine, and a lake that
shone like burnished silver. Between the hills
there lay a field of ripe barley.

The fairy then dropped three drops of the
green liquid in the woman's right eye, and said:
"Look now."

The woman looked, and she saw men and
women she had known in times past, cutting the
barley and gathering fruit from the trees.

She cried out: "I see many who once lived on

earth and have long been dead. What are they doing here?"

Said the fairy: "These people are suffering punishment for their evil deeds."

When she had spoken thus, the fairy woman passed her hand over the woman's eyes, and the vision of green hills and harvest fields and reapers vanished at once. She found herself standing once more in the bare, dimly-lighted chamber. Then the fairy gave her gifts of cloth and healing ointments, and, leading her to the door, bade her farewell. The door opened, the turf was lifted up, and the woman left the fairy's dwelling and returned to her own home.

For a time she kept the power of seeing the fairies as they went to and fro near her house. But one day she spoke to one of them, and the fairy asked: "With which eye do you see me?"

Said the woman: "I see you with both my eyes."

The fairy breathed on her eyes, and then was lost to sight. Never again did the woman behold the fairies, for the power that had been given her was taken away from her eyes by this fairy to whom she had spoken.

CHAPTER X

The Story of Michael Scott

Michael Scott, who lived during the thirteenth century, was known far and near as a great scholar, and it is told that he had dealings with the fairies and other spirits. When he wanted to erect a house or a bridge he called the " wee folk " to his aid, and they did the work for him in a single night. He had great skill as a healer of wounds and curer of diseases, and the people called him a magician.

When Michael was a young man he set out on a journey to Edinburgh with two companions. They travelled on foot, and one day, when they were climbing a high hill, they sat down to rest. No sooner had they done so than they heard a loud hissing sound. They looked in the direction whence the sound came, and saw with horror a great white serpent, curved in wheel shape, rolling towards them at a rapid speed. It was evident that the monster was going to attack them, and when it began to roll up the hill-side as swiftly as it had crossed the moor, Michael's two companions sprang to their feet and ran away, shouting with terror. Michael was a man who knew no fear, and he made up his mind to attack the serpent. He stood waiting for it, with his staff firmly grasped in his right hand.

When the serpent came close to Michael it uncurved its body and, throwing itself into a coil, raised its head to strike, its jaws gaping wide and its forked tongue thrust out like an arrow. Michael at once raised his staff, and struck the monster so fierce a blow that he cut its body into three parts. Then he turned away, and called upon his friends to wait for him. They heard his voice, stopped running, and gazed upon him with wonder as he walked towards them very calmly and at an easy pace. It was a great relief to them to learn from Michael that he had slain the fearsome monster.

They walked on together, and had not gone far when they came to a house in which lived a wise old woman. As the sun was beginning to set and it would soon be dark, they asked her for a night's lodging, and she invited them to enter the house. One of the men then told her of their adventure with the wheeling serpent which Michael had slain.

Said the Wise Woman: "Are you sure the white serpent is dead?"

"It must be dead," Michael answered, "because I cut its body into three parts."

Said the Wise Woman: "This white serpent is no ordinary serpent. It has power to unite the severed parts of its body again. Once before it was attacked by a brave man, who cut it in two. The head part of its body, however, crawled to a stream. After bathing in the stream it crawled back and joined itself to the tail part. The serpent then became whole again, and once more it bathed in the healing waters of the stream. All serpents do this after attacking a human being. If a man who has been stung by a serpent should hasten to the stream before the serpent can reach it, he will be cured and the serpent will die."

"You have great knowledge of the mysteries," Michael exclaimed with wonder.

Said the Wise Woman: "You have overcome the white serpent this time, but you may not be so fortunate when next it comes against you. Be assured of this: the serpent will, after it has been healed, lie in wait for you to take vengeance. When next it attacks, you will receive no warning that it is near."

"I shall never cross the high mountain again," Michael declared.

Said the Wise Woman: "The serpent will search for you and find you, no matter where you may be."

"Alas!" Michael exclaimed, "evil is my fate. What can I do to protect myself against the serpent?"

Said the Wise Woman: "Go now to the place where you smote the serpent, and carry away the middle part of its body. Make haste, lest you be too late."

Michael took her advice, and asked his companions to go with him; but they were afraid to do so, and he set out alone.

He walked quickly, and soon came to the place where he had struck down the monster. He found the middle part and the tail part of the white serpent's body, but the head part was nowhere to be seen. He knew then that the woman had spoken truly, and, as darkness was coming on, he did not care to search for the stream to which the head part had gone. Lifting up the middle part of the body, which still quivered, he hastened back towards the house of the Wise Woman. The sky darkened, and the stars began to appear. Michael grew uneasy. He felt sure that something was following him at a distance, so he quickened his steps and never looked back. At length he reached the house in safety, and he was glad to find that there were charms above the door which prevented any evil spirit from entering.

The Wise Woman welcomed Michael, and

asked him to give her the part of the serpent's body which he had brought with him. He did so willingly, and she thanked him, and said: "Now I shall prepare a meal for you and your companions."

The woman at once set to work and cooked an excellent meal. Michael began to wonder why she showed him and his friends so much kindness and why she was in such high spirits. She laughed and talked as merrily as a girl, and he suspected she had been made happy because he had brought her the middle part of the white serpent's body. He resolved to watch her and find out, if possible, what she was going to do with it.

After eating his supper Michael pretended that he suffered from pain, and went into the kitchen to sit beside the fire. He told the woman that the heat took away the pain, and asked her to allow him to sleep in a chair in front of the fire. She said, "Very well," so he sat down, while his weary companions went to bed. The woman put a pot on the fire, and placed in it the middle part of the serpent's body.

Michael took note of this, but said nothing. He pretended to sleep. The part of the serpent began to frizzle in the pot, and the woman came from another room, lifted off the lid, and looked in. Then she touched the cut of the serpent with her right finger. When she did so a cock crew on the roof of the house.   Michael was startled.   He opened his eyes and looked round.

Said the Wise Woman: " I thought you were fast asleep."

" I cannot sleep because of the pain I suffer," Michael told her.

Said the Wise Woman: " If you cannot sleep, you may be of service to me.   I am very weary and wish to sleep.   I am cooking the part of the serpent.   Watch the pot for me, and see that the part does not burn.   Call me when it is properly cooked, but be sure not to touch it before you do so."

" I shall not sleep," Michael said, " so I may as well have something to do."

The Wise Woman smiled, and said: " After you call me, I shall cure your trouble."   Then she went to her bed and lay down to sleep.

Michael sat watching the pot, and when he found that the portion of the serpent's body was fully cooked, he lifted the pot off the fire.   Before calling the old woman, he thought he would first do what she had done when she lifted the lid off the pot.   He dipped his finger into the juice of the serpent's body.   The tip of his right finger was badly burned, so he thrust it into his mouth. The cock on the roof flapped its wings at once, and crowed so loudly that the old woman woke up in bed and screamed.

Michael felt that there must be magic in the juice of the serpent. New light and knowledge broke in upon him, and he discovered that he had the power to foretell events, to work magic cures, and to read the minds of other people.

The old woman came out of her room. "You did not call me," she said in a sad voice.

Michael knew what she meant. Had he called her, she would have been the first to taste the juice of the white serpent and receive from it the great power he now himself possessed.

"I slew the serpent," he said, "and had the first right to taste of its juice."

Said the Wise Woman: "I dare not scold you now. Nor need I tell you what powers you possess, for you have become wiser than I am. You can cure diseases, you can foretell and foresee what is to take place, you have power to make the fairies obey your commands, and you can obtain greater knowledge about the hidden mysteries than any other man alive. All that I ask of you is your friendship."

"I give you my friendship willingly," Michael said to her. Then the Wise Woman sat down beside him and asked him many questions about hidden things, and Michael found himself able to answer each one. They sat together talking until dawn. Then Michael awoke his companions, and the woman cooked a breakfast. When

Michael bade her good-bye, she said: " Do not forget me, for you owe much to me."

" I shall never forget you," he promised her.

Michael and his companions resumed their journey. They walked until sunset, but did not reach a house.

" To-night," one of the men said, " we must sleep on the heather."

Michael smiled. "To-night," said he, "we shall sleep in Edinburgh."

" It is still a day's journey from here," the man reminded him.

Michael laid his staff on the ground and said: " Let us three sit on this staff and see how we fare."

His companions laughed, and sat down as he asked them to do. They thought it a great joke.

" Hold tight!" Michael advised them. The men, still amused, grasped the staff in their hands and held it tightly.

" Staff of mine!" Michael cried, "carry us to Edinburgh."

No sooner did he speak than the staff rose high in the air. The men were terror-stricken as the staff flew towards the clouds and then went forward with the speed of lightning. They shivered with fear and with cold. Snow-flakes fell on them as the staff flew across the sky, for they were higher up than the peak of Ben Nevis. When night was falling and the stars came out one by one, the staff began to descend.   Happy were Michael's companions when they came down safely on the outskirts of Edinburgh.

They walked into the town in silence, and the first man they met stood and gazed with wonder upon them in the lamplight.

"Why do you stare at strangers?" Michael asked.

Said the man: "There is snow on your caps and your shoulders."

Having spoken thus, a sudden fear overcame him, and he turned and fled, believing that the three strangers were either wizards or fairies.

Michael shook the snow off his cap and shoulders, and his companions did the same. They then sought out a lodging, and having eaten their suppers, went to bed.

Next morning Michael found that his companions had risen early and gone away. He knew that they were afraid of him, so he smiled and said to himself: "I bear them no ill-will. I prefer now to be alone."

Michael soon became famous as a builder. When he was asked to build a house, he called the fairies to his aid, and they did the work in the night-time for him.

Once he was travelling towards Inverness, and

came to a river which was in flood. The ford could not be crossed, and several men stood beside it looking across the deep turbid waters. "It is a pity," one said to Michael, "there is no bridge here."

Said Michael: "I have come to build a bridge, and my workers will begin to erect it to-night."

Those who heard him laughed and turned away, but great was their surprise next morning to find that a bridge had been built. They crossed over it with their horses and cattle, and as they went on their way they spread the fame of Michael far and wide.

As time went on Michael found that his fairy workers wished to do more than he required of them. They began to visit him every evening, crying out: "Work! work! work!"

So Michael thought one day that he would set them to perform a task beyond their powers, and when next they came to him crying out: "Work! work! work!" he told them to close up the Inverness firth and cut it off from the sea. The fairies at once hastened away to obey his command.

Michael thought of the swift tides and of the great volume of water flowing down from the rivers by night and by day, and was certain that the fairies would not be able to close the firth.

Next morning, however, he found that the river Ness was rising rapidly, and threatening to flood the town of Inverness.   He climbed a hill and looked seaward.   Then he found that the fairies had very nearly finished the work he had set them to do.   They had made two long promontories which jutted across the firth, and there remained only a narrow space through which the water surged.   The incoming tide kept back the waters flowing from the river, and that was why the Ness was rising in flood.   Not until after the tide turned did the waters of the river begin to fall.

Michael summoned his fairy workers that evening, and ordered them to open up the firth again. They hastened away to obey him, and after darkness came on they began to destroy the promontories.   The moon rose as they went on with their work.   A holy man walking along the shore saw the fairies, and prayed for protection against them.   When he did so the fairies fled away, and were unable again to visit the promontories, and so these still lie jutting across the firth like crab's toes.   The one has been named Chanonry Point, and on the peninsula opposite it there now stands Fort George, which was placed there to prevent enemy ships from sailing up to Inverness.

When the fairies found they were unable to complete their task they returned to Michael, crying out again: "Work! work! work!"

Michael then thought of an impossible task which would keep them busy. He said: "Go and make rope-ladders that will reach to the back of the moon. They must be made of sea sand and white foam."

The fairies hastened away to obey his command. They could not, however, make the ropes for Michael, try as they might.

Some say that Michael's workers are still attempting to carry out the work he last set them to do, and that is why wreaths of foam and ropes of twisted sand are sometimes found on the sea-shore till this day.

It is told that one weak-minded and clumsy old fairy man used to spend night after night trying to make ropes of sand and foam on the shore of Kirkcaldy Bay. When he grew weary he lay down to rest himself, and on cold nights he could be heard moaning: "My toes are cold, my toes are cold."

CHAPTER XI

In the Kingdom of Seals

The sea fairies have grey skin-coverings and resemble seals. They dwell in cave houses on the borders of Land-under-Waves, where they have a kingdom of their own. They love music and the dance, like the green land fairies, and when harper or piper plays on the beach they come up to listen, their sloe-black eyes sparkling with joy. On moonlight nights they hear the mermaids singing on the rocks when human beings are fast asleep, and they call to them: "Sing again the old sea croons; sing again!" All night long the sea fairies call thus when mermaids cease to sing, and the mermaids sing again and again to them. When the wind pipes loud and free, and the sea leaps and whirls and swings and cries aloud with wintry merriment, the sea fairies dance with the dancing waves, tossing white petals of foam over their heads, and twining pearls of spray about their necks. They love to hunt the silvern salmon in the forests of sea-

SEAL-FOLK LISTENING TO A MERMAID'S SONG

From a drawing by John Duncan, A.R.S.A.

tangle and in ocean's deep blue glens, and far up dark ravines through which flow rivers of sweet mountain waters gemmed with stars.

The sea fairies have a language of their own, and they are also skilled in human speech. When they come ashore they can take the forms of men or women, and turn billows into dark horses with grey manes and long grey tails, and on these they ride over mountain and moor.

There was once a fisherman who visited the palace of the queen of sea fairies, and told on his return all he had seen and all he had heard. He dwelt in a little township nigh to John-o'-Groat's House, and was wont to catch fish and seals. When he found that he could earn much money by hunting seals, whose skins make warm winter clothing, he troubled little about catching salmon or cod, and worked constantly as a seal-hunter. He crept among the rocks searching for his prey, and visited lonely seal-haunted islands across the Pentland Firth, where he often found the strange sea-prowlers lying on smooth flat ledges of rock fast asleep in the warm sunshine.

In his house he had great bundles of dried sealskins, and people came from a distance to purchase them from him. His fame as a seal-hunter went far and wide.

One evening a dark stranger rode up to his house, mounted on a black, spirited mare with grey

mane and grey tail.   He called to the fisherman
who came out, and then said: "Make haste and
ride with me towards the east.   My master desires
to do business with you."

"I have no horse," the fisherman answered,
"but I shall walk to your master's house on the
morrow."

Said the stranger: "Come now.   Ride with
me.   My good mare is fleet-footed and strong."

"As you will," answered the fisherman, who at
once mounted the mare behind the stranger.

The mare turned round and right-about, and
galloped eastward faster than the wind of March.
Shingle rose in front of her like rock-strewn sea-
spray, and a sand-cloud gathered and swept out
behind like mountain mists that are scattered
before a gale.   The fisherman gasped for breath,
for although the wind was blowing against his
back when he mounted the mare, it blew fiercely
in his face as he rode on.   The mare went fast
and far until she drew nigh to a precipice.   Near
the edge of it she halted suddenly.   The fisherman found then that the wind was still blowing
seaward, although he had thought it had veered
round as he rode.   Never before had he sat on
the back of so fleet-footed a mare.

Said the stranger: "We have almost reached
my master's dwelling."

The fisherman looked round about him with

surprise, and saw neither house nor the smoke of one.   " Where is your master?" he asked.

Said the stranger: "You shall see him presently.   Come with me."

As he spoke he walked towards the edge of the precipice and looked over.   The fisherman did the same, and saw nothing but the grey lonely sea heaving in a long slow swell, and sea-birds wheeling and sliding down the wind.

"Where is your master?" he asked once again.

With that the stranger suddenly clasped the seal-hunter in his arms, and crying, "Come with me," leapt over the edge of the precipice.   The mare leapt with her master.

Down, down they fell through the air, scattering the startled sea-birds.   Screaming and fluttering, the birds rose in clouds about and above them, and down ever down the men and the mare continued to fall till they plunged into the sea, and sank and sank, while the light around them faded into darkness deeper than night.   The fisherman wondered to find himself still alive as he passed through the sea depths, seeing naught, hearing naught, and still moving swiftly.   At length he ceased to sink, and went forward.   He suffered no pain or discomfort, nor was he afraid.   His only feeling was of wonder, and in the thick, cool darkness he wondered greatly what would happen next. At length he saw a faint green light, and as he went onward the light grew brighter and brighter, until the glens and bens and forests of the sea kingdom arose before his eyes. Then he discovered that he was swimming beside the stranger and that they had both been changed into seals.

Said the stranger: "Yonder is my master's house."

The fisherman looked, and saw a township of foam-white houses on the edge of a great sea-forest and fronted by a bank of sea-moss which was green as grass but more beautiful, and very bright. There were crowds of seal-folk in the township. He saw them moving about to and fro, and heard their voices, but he could not understand their speech. Mothers nursed their babes, and young children played games on banks of green sea-moss, and from the brown and golden sea-forest came sounds of music and the shouts of dancers.

Said the stranger: "Here is my master's house. Let us enter."

He led the fisherman towards the door of a great foam-white palace with its many bright windows. It was thatched with red tangle, and the door was of green stone. The door opened as smoothly as a summer wave that moves across a river mouth, and the fisherman entered with his guide. He found himself in a dimly-lighted room, and saw an old grey seal stretched on a bed, and heard him moaning with pain. Beside the bed lay a blood-stained knife, and the fisherman knew at a glance that it was his own. Then he remembered that, not many hours before, he had stabbed a seal, and that it had escaped by plunging into the sea, carrying the knife in its back.

The fisherman was startled to realize that the old seal on the bed was the very one he had tried to kill, and his heart was filled with fear. He threw himself down and begged for forgiveness and mercy, for he feared that he would be put to death.

The guide lifted up the knife and asked: "Have you ever seen this knife before?" He spoke in human language.

"That is my knife, alas!" exclaimed the fisherman.

Said the guide: "The wounded seal is my father. Our doctors are unable to cure him. They can do naught without your help. That is why I visited your house and urged you to come with me. I ask your pardon for deceiving you, O man! but as I love my father greatly, I had to do as I have done."

"Do not ask my pardon," the fisherman said; "I have need of yours. I am sorry and ashamed for having stabbed your father."

Said the guide: "Lay your hand on the wound and wish it to be healed."

The fisherman laid his hand on the wound, and the pain that the seal suffered passed into his hand, but did not remain long. As if by magic, the wound was healed at once. Then the old grey seal rose up strong and well again.

Said the guide: "You have served us well this day, O man!"

When the fisherman had entered the house, all the seals that were within were weeping tears of sorrow, but they ceased to weep as soon as he had laid his hand on the wound, and when the old seal rose up they all became merry and bright.

The fisherman wondered what would happen next. For a time the seals seemed to forget his presence, but at length his guide spoke to him and said: "Now, O man! you can return to your own home where your wife and children await you. I shall lead you through the sea depths, and take you on my mare across the plain which we crossed when coming hither."

"I give you thanks," the fisherman exclaimed.

Said the guide: "Before you leave there is one thing you must do; you must take a vow never again to hunt seals."

The fisherman answered: "Surely, I promise never again to hunt for seals."

Said the guide: "If ever you break your promise you shall die. I counsel you to keep it, and as long as you do so you will prosper. Every time you set lines, or cast a net, you will catch much fish. Our seal-servants will help you, and if you wish to reward them for their services, take with you in your boat a harp or pipe and play sweet music, for music is the delight of all seals."

The fisherman vowed he would never break his promise, and the guide then led him back to dry land. As soon as he reached the shore he ceased to be a seal and became a man once again. The guide, who had also changed shape, breathed over a great wave and, immediately, it became a dark mare with grey mane and grey tail. He then mounted the mare, and bade the fisherman mount behind him. The mare rose in the air as lightly as wind-tossed spray, and passing through the clouds of startled sea-birds reached the top of the precipice. On she raced at once, raising the shingle in front and a cloud of sand behind. The night was falling and the stars began to appear, but it was not quite dark when the fisherman's house was reached.

The fisherman dismounted, and his guide spoke and said: "Take this from me, and may you live happily."

He handed the fisherman a small bag, and crying: "Farewell! Remember your vow," he wheeled his mare right round and passed swiftly out of sight.

The fisherman entered his house, and found his wife still there. "You have returned," she said. "How did you fare?"

"I know not yet," he answered. Then he sat down and opened the bag, and to his surprise and delight found it was full of pearls.

His wife uttered a cry of wonder, and said: "From whom did you receive this treasure?"

The fisherman then related all that had taken place, and his wife wondered to hear him.

"Never again will I hunt seals," he exclaimed. And he kept his word and prospered, and lived happily until the day of his death.

CHAPTER XII

Story of Thomas the Rhymer

At the beginning of each summer, when the milk-white hawthorn is in bloom, anointing the air with its sweet odour, and miles and miles of golden whin adorn the glens and hill-slopes, the fairies come forth in grand procession, headed by the Fairy Queen. They are mounted on little white horses, and when on a night of clear soft moonlight the people hear the clatter of many hoofs, the jingling of bridles, and the sound of laughter and sweet music coming sweetly down the wind, they whisper one to another: " 'Tis the Fairy Folks' Raid", or " Here come the Riders of the Shee".

The Fairy Queen, who rides in front, is gowned in grass-green silk, and wears over her shoulders a mantle of green velvet adorned with silver spangles. She is of great beauty. Her eyes are like wood violets, her teeth like pearls, her brow and neck are swan-white, and her cheeks bloom like ripe apples. Her long clustering hair of rich auburn gold which falls over her shoulders and down her back, is bound round about with a snood that glints with star-like gems, and there is one great flashing jewel above her brow. On each lock of her horse's mane hang sweet-toned silver bells that tinkle merrily as she rides on.

The riders who follow her in couples are likewise clad in green, and wear little red caps bright as the flaming poppies in waving fields of yellow barley. Their horses' manes are hung with silver whistles upon which the soft winds play. Some fairies twang harps of gold, some make sweet music on oaten pipes, and some sing with birdlike voices in the moonlight. When song and music cease, they chat and laugh merrily as they ride on their way. Over hills and down glens they go, but no hoof-mark is left by their horses. So lightly do the little white creatures trot that not a grass blade is broken by their tread, nor is the honey-dew spilled from blue harebells and yellow buttercups. Sometimes the fairies ride over tree-tops or through the air on eddies of western wind. The Riders of the Shee always come from the west.

When the Summer Fairy Raid is coming, the people hang branches of rowan over their doors and round their rooms, and when the Winter Raid is coming they hang up holly and mistletoe as protection from attack; for sometimes the fairies steal pretty children while they lie fast asleep, and carry them off to Fairyland, and sometimes they lure away pipers and bards, and women who have sweet singing voices.

Once there was a great bard who was called Thomas the Rhymer. He lived at Ercildoune (Earlston), in Berwickshire, during the thirteenth century. It is told that he vanished for seven years, and that when he reappeared he had the gift of prophecy. Because he was able to foretell events, he was given the name of True Thomas.

All through Scotland, from the Cheviot Hills to the Pentland Firth, the story of Thomas the Rhymer has long been known.

During his seven years' absence from home he is said to have dwelt in fairyland. One evening, so runs the tale, he was walking alone on the banks of Leader Water when he saw riding towards him the Fairy Queen on her milk-white steed, the silver bells tinkling on its mane, and the silver bridle jingling sweet and clear. He was amazed at her beauty, and thinking she was the Queen of Heaven, bared his head and knelt before her as she dismounted, saying: "All hail, mighty Queen of Heaven! I have never before seen your equal."

Said the green-clad lady: "Ah! Thomas, you have named me wrongly. I am the Queen of Fairyland, and have come to visit you."

"What seek you with me?" Thomas asked.

Said the Fairy Queen: "You must hasten at once to Fairyland, and serve me there for seven years."

Then she laid a spell upon him, and he had to obey her will. She mounted her milk-white steed and Thomas mounted behind her, and they rode off together. They crossed the Leader Water, and the horse went swifter than the wind over hill and dale until a great wide desert was reached. No house nor human being could be seen anywhere. East and west, north and south, the level desert stretched as far as eye could see. They rode on and on until at length the Fairy Queen spoke, and said: "Dismount, O Thomas, and I shall show you three wonders."

Thomas dismounted and the Fairy Queen dismounted also. Said she: "Look, yonder is a narrow road full of thorns and briers. That is the path to Heaven. Yonder is a broad highway which runs across a lily lea. That is the path of wickedness. Yonder is another road. It twines round the hill-side towards the west. That is the way to Fairyland, and you and I must ride thither."

Again she mounted her milk-white steed and Thomas mounted behind. They rode on and on, crossing many rivers. Nor sun or moon could be seen nor any stars, and in the silence and thick darkness they heard the deep voice of the roaring sea.

At length a light appeared in front of them, which grew larger and brighter as they rode on. Then Thomas saw a beautiful country. The horse halted and he found himself in the midst of a green garden. When they had dismounted, the Fairy Queen plucked an apple and gave it to Thomas, saying: " This is your reward for coming with me. After you have eaten of it you will have power to speak truly of coming events, and men will know you as ' True Thomas '."

Thomas ate the apple and then followed the queen to her palace. He was given clothing of green silk and shoes of green velvet, and he dwelt among the fairies for seven years. The time passed so quickly that the seven years seemed no longer than seven hours.

After his return to Ercildoune, where he lived in a castle, Thomas made many songs and ballads and pronounced in rhyme many prophecies. He travelled up and down the country, and wherever he went he foretold events, some of which took place while yet he lived among men, but others did not happen until long years afterwards. There are still some prophecies which are as yet unfulfilled.

It is said that when Thomas was an old man the Fairy Queen returned for him. One day, as he stood chatting with knights and ladies, she rode from the river-side and called: "True Thomas, your time has come."

Thomas cried to his friends: "Farewell, all of you, I shall return no more." Then he mounted the milk-white steed behind the Fairy Queen, and galloped across the ford. Several knights leapt into their saddles and followed the Rider of the Shee, but when they reached the opposite bank of the river they could see naught of Thomas and the Fairy Queen.

It is said that Thomas still dwells in Fairyland, and that he goes about among the Riders of the Shee when they come forth at the beginning of each summer. Those who have seen him ride past tell that he looks very old, and that his hair and long beard are white as driven snow. At other times he goes about invisible, except when he attends a market to buy horses for a fairy army which is to take part in a great battle. He drives the horses to Fairyland and keeps them there. When he has collected a sufficient number, it is told, he will return again to wage war against the invaders of his country, whom he will defeat on the banks of the Clyde.

Thomas wanders far and wide through Scotland. He has been seen, folks have told, riding out of a fairy dwelling below Eildon Hills, from another fairy dwelling below Dumbuck Hill, near Dumbarton, and from a third fairy dwelling below the boat-shaped mound of Tom-na-hurich at Inverness.

Once a man who climbed Dumbuck Hill came to an open door and entered through it. In a dim chamber he saw a little old man resting on his elbow, who spoke to him and said: " Has the time come?"

The man was stricken with fear and fled away. When he pressed through the doorway, the door shut behind him, and turf closed over it.

Another story about Thomas is told at Inverness. Two fiddlers, named Farquhar Grant and Thomas Cumming, natives of Strathspey, who lived over three hundred years ago, once visited Inverness during the Christmas season. They hoped to earn money by their music, and as soon as they arrived in the town began to show their skill in the streets. Although they had great fame as fiddlers in Strathspey, they found that the townspeople took little notice of them. When night fell, they had not collected enough money to buy food for supper and to pay for a night's lodging. They stopped playing and went, with their fiddles under their right arms, towards the wooden bridge that then crossed the River Ness.

Just as they were about to walk over the bridge they saw a little old man coming towards them in the dusk. His beard was very long and very white, but although his back was bent his step was easy and light. He stopped in front of the fiddlers, and, much to their surprise, hailed them by their names saying: "How fares it with you, my merry fiddlers?"

"Badly, badly!" answered Grant.

"Very badly indeed!" Cumming said.

"Come with me," said the old man. "I have need of fiddlers to-night, and will reward you well. A great ball is to be held in my castle, and there are no musicians."

Grant and Cumming were glad to get the chance of earning money by playing their fiddles and said they would go. "Then follow me and make haste," said the old man. The fiddlers followed him across the wooden bridge and across the darkening moor beyond. He walked with rapid strides, and sometimes the fiddlers had to break into a run to keep up with him. Now and again that strange, nimble old man would turn round and cry: "Are you coming, my merry fiddlers?"

"We are doing our best," Grant would answer, while Cumming muttered: "By my faith, old man, but you walk quickly!"

"Make haste, Grant; make haste, Cumming," the old man would then exclaim; "my guests will be growing impatient."

In time they reached the big boat-shaped

mound called Tom-na-hurich, and the old man began to climb it. The fiddlers followed at a short distance. Then he stopped suddenly and stamped the ground three times with his right foot. A door opened and a bright light streamed forth.

"Here is my castle, Cumming; here is my castle, Grant," exclaimed the old man, who was no other than Thomas the Rhymer. "Come within and make merry."

The fiddlers paused for a moment at the open door, but Thomas the Rhymer drew from his belt a purse of gold and made it jingle. "This purse holds your wages," he told them. "First you will get your share of the feast, then you will give us fine music."

As the fiddlers were as hungry as they were poor, they could not resist the offer made to them, and entered the fairy castle. As soon as they entered, the door was shut behind them.

They found themselves in a great hall, which was filled with brilliant light. Tables were spread with all kinds of food, and guests sat round them eating and chatting and laughing merrily.

Thomas led the fiddlers to a side table, and two graceful maidens clad in green came forward with dishes of food and bottles of wine, and said: "Eat and drink to your hearts' content, Farquhar Grant and Thomas Cumming—Farquhar o' Feshie

and Thomas o' Tom-an-Torran.   You are welcome here to-night."

The fiddlers wondered greatly that the maidens
knew not only their personal names but even the
names of their homes.   They began to eat, and,
no matter how much they ate, the food on the
table did not seem to grow less.   They poured
out wine, but they could not empty the bottles.

Said Cumming: "This is a feast indeed."

Said Grant: "There was never such a feast in
Strathspey."

When the feast was ended the fiddlers were led
to the ballroom, and there they began to play
merry music for the gayest and brightest and
happiest dancers they ever saw before.   They
played reels and jigs and strathspeys, and yet
never grew weary.   The dancers praised their
music, and fair girls brought them fruit and wine
at the end of each dance.   If the guests were
happy, the musicians were happier still, and they
were sorry to find at length that the ball was
coming to an end.   How long it had lasted they
could not tell.   When the dancers began to go
away they were still unwearied and willing to go
on playing.

Thomas the Rhymer entered the ballroom, and
spoke to the fiddlers, saying: "You have done
well, my merry men.   I will lead you to the door,
and pay you for your fine music."

The fiddlers were sorry to go away. At the door Thomas the Rhymer divided the purse of gold between them, and asked: "Are you satisfied?"

"Satisfied!" Cumming repeated. "Oh, yes, for you and your guests have been very kind!"

"We should gladly come back again," Grant said.

When they had left the castle the fiddlers found that it was bright day. The sun shone from an unclouded sky, and the air was warm. As they walked on they were surprised to see fields of ripe corn, which was a strange sight at the Christmas season. Then they came to the riverside, and found instead of a wooden bridge a new stone bridge with seven arches.

"This stone bridge was not here last night," Cumming said.

"Not that I saw," said Grant.

When they crossed the bridge they found that the town of Inverness had changed greatly. Many new houses had been built; there were even new streets. The people they saw moving about wore strange clothing. One spoke to the fiddlers, and asked: "Who are you, and whence come you?"

They told him their names, and said that on the previous night they had played their fiddles at a great ball in a castle near the town.

The man smiled. Then Farquhar said: "The bridge we crossed over last evening was made of wood. Now you have a bridge of stone. Have the fairies built it for you?"

The man laughed, and exclaimed, as he turned away: "You are mad. The stone bridge was built before I was born."

Boys began to collect round the fiddlers. They jeered at their clothing, and cried: "Go back to the madhouse you have escaped from."

The fiddlers hastened out of the town, and took the road which leads to Strathspey. Men who passed them stopped and looked back, but they spoke to no one, and scarcely spoke, indeed, to one another.

Darkness came on, and they crept into an empty, half-ruined house by the wayside and slept there. How long they slept they knew not, but when they came out again they saw that the harvesting had begun. Fields were partly cut, but no workers could be seen in them, although the sun was already high in the heavens. They drank water from a well, and went on their way, until at length they reached their native village. They entered it joyfully, but were unable to find their homes. There, too, new houses had been built, and strange faces were seen. They heard a bell ringing, and then knew it was Sabbath day, and they walked towards the church. A man

spoke to them near the gate of the churchyard
and said: "You are strangers here."

"No, indeed, we are not strangers," Grant
assured him. "This is our native village."

"You must have left it long ago," said the man,
"for I have lived here all my life, and I do not
know you."

Then Grant told his name and that of his companion, and the names of their fathers and mothers.
"We are fine fiddlers," he added; "our equal is
not to be found north of the Grampians."

Said the man: "Ah! you are the two men my
grandfather used to speak of. He never saw you,
but he heard his father tell that you had been
decoyed by Thomas the Rhymer, who took you
to Tom-na-hurich. Your friends mourned for
you greatly, but now you are quite forgotten, for
it is fully a hundred years since you went away
from here."

The fiddlers thought that the man was mocking
them, and turned their backs upon him. They
went into the churchyard, and began to read the
names on the gravestones. They saw stones
erected to their wives and children, and to their
children's children, and gazed on them with amaze-
ment, taking no notice of the people who passed
by to the church door.

At length they entered the church hand in
hand, with their fiddles under their arms. They

stood for a brief space at the doorway, gazing at the congregation, but were unable to recognize a single face among the people who looked round at them.

The minister was in the pulpit. He had been told who the strangers were, and, after gazing for a moment in silence, he began to pray. No sooner did he do so than the two fiddlers crumbled into dust.

Such is the story of the two fiddlers who spent a hundred years in a fairy dwelling, thinking they had played music there for but a single night.

CHAPTER XIII

The Maid-of-the-Wave

The mermaid, or, as she is called in Gaelic, Maid-of-the-Wave, has great beauty and is sweet-voiced. Half her body is of fish shape, and glitters like a salmon in sunshine, and she has long copper-coloured hair which she loves to comb as she sits on a rock on a lonely shore, gazing in a mirror of silver, and singing a song in praise of her own great beauty. Sometimes, on moonlight nights, she takes off her skin covering and puts on sea-blue garments, and then she seems fairer than any lady in the land.

Once a young crofter was wandering below the cliffs on a beautiful summer night when the wind was still and the silver moon shone through the clear depths of ocean, casting a flood of light through Land-under-Waves. He heard sounds of song and laughter. He crept softly towards a shadowy rock, and, climbing it, looked down on a bank of white sand. There he beheld a company of mermaids dancing in a ring round a maid who was fairest of the fair. They had taken off their skin coverings, and were gowned in pale blue, and, as they wheeled round about, their copper tresses streamed out behind their backs, glistening in the moonlight. He was delighted by their singing and amazed at their beauty.

At length he crept stealthily down the rock, and ran towards the skin coverings lying on the sand. He seized one and ran off with it. When the mermaids saw him they screamed and scattered in confusion, and snatching up their skin coverings, leapt into the sea and vanished from sight. One maid remained behind. This was the fair one round whom the others had been dancing. Her skin covering was gone, and so she could not return to her sea home.

Meanwhile the crofter ran to his house and hid the skin covering in a box, which he locked, placing the key in his pocket. He wondered what would happen next, and he had not long to wait. Some-one came to his door and knocked softly. He stood listening in silence. Then he heard the knocking again, and opened the door. A Maid-of-the-Wave, clad in pale sea-blue garments, stood before him, the moonlight glistening on her wet copper hair. Tears stood in her soft blue eyes as she spoke sweetly saying: "O man, have pity and give me back my skin covering so that I may return to my sea home."

She was so gentle and so beautiful that the

crofter did not wish her to go away, so he answered: "What I have got I keep. Do not sorrow, O fair one. Remain here and be my bride."

The mermaid turned away and wandered along the shore, but the crofter did not leave his house. In the morning she returned again, and the crofter said to her: "Be my bride."

The mermaid consented saying: "I cannot return to my fair sea home. I must live now among human beings, and I know no one except you alone. Be kind to me, but do not tell man or woman who I am or whence I came."

The crofter promised to keep her secret, and that day they were married. All the people of the township loved Maid-of-the-Wave, and rejoiced to have her among them. They thought she was a princess from a far country who had been carried away by the fairies.

For seven years the crofter and his wife lived happily together. They had three children, two boys and a girl, and Maid-of-the-Wave loved them dearly.

When the seventh year was drawing to a close the crofter set out on a journey to Big Town, having business to do there. His wife was lonely without him, and sat often on the shore singing songs to her baby girl and gazing over the sea.

One evening, as she wandered amidst the rocks, her eldest boy, whose name was Kenneth, came

to her and said: "I found a key which opened
Father's box, and in the box I saw a skin like the
skin of a salmon, but brighter and more beautiful,
and very large."

His mother gasped with surprise and secret joy,
and asked softly: "Will you give me the key?"

Kenneth handed the key to her, and she hid it
in her bosom. Then she said: "It is getting
late. The moon will not rise till near midnight.
Come home, little Kenneth, and I shall make
supper, and put you to bed, and sing you to
sleep."

As she spoke she began to sing a joyous song,
and Kenneth was glad that his mother was no
longer sad because his father was from home. He
grasped his mother's hand, and tripped lightly by
her side as they went homeward together.

When the two boys had supper, and were
slumbering in bed, the crofter's wife hushed her
girl-baby to sleep, and laid her in her cradle.
Then she took the key from her bosom and
opened the box. There she found her long-lost
skin covering. She wished to return to her fair
sea home, yet she did not care to leave her
children. She sat by the fire for a time, wondering
if she should put on the skin covering or place it
in the box again. At length, however, she heard
the sound of singing coming over the waves, and
the song she heard was like this:—

Maid-of-the-Wave, the dew mist is falling,
  Thy sisters are calling and longing for thee;
Maid-of-the-Wave, the white stars are gleaming,
  Their bright rays are streaming across the dark sea.
Maid-of-the-Wave, would thou wert near us!
  Come now to cheer us—Oh, hear us! Oh, hear us!

Maid-of-the-Wave, a sea-wind is blowing,
  The tide at its flowing hath borne us to thee;
Maid-of-the-Wave, the tide is now turning—
  Oh! we are all yearning our sister to see.
Maid-of-the-Wave, come back and ne'er leave us,
  The loss of thee grieves us—believe us! believe us!

Maid-of-the-Wave, what caredst thou in childhood
  For moorland or wildwood? thy home was the sea.
Maid-of-the-Wave, thine exile and sorrow
  Will end ere the morrow, and thou shalt be free.
Maid-of-the-Wave, to-night from our sea-halls
  A heart-spell on thee falls—the sea calls! the sea calls!

She kissed the two boys and wept over them.
Then she knelt beside her little baby girl, who
smiled in her sleep, and sang:

> Sleep, oh! sleep my fair, my rare one,
>   Sleep, oh! sleep nor sigh nor fret thee.
> Though I leave thee it doth grieve me—
>   Ne'er, oh! ne'er will I forget thee.
>
> Sleep, oh! sleep, my white, my bright one,
>   Sleep, oh! sleep and know no sorrow.
> Soft I kiss thee, I who'll miss thee
>   And thy sire who'll come to-morrow.
>
> Sleep, oh! sleep my near, my dear one,
>   While thy brothers sleep beside thee.
> They will waken all forsaken—
>   Fare-thee-well, and woe betide me!

When she had sung this song she heard voices from the sea calling low and calling sweet:

> Maid-of-the-Wave, oh! list to our singing;
>   The white moon is winging its way o'er the sea.
> Maid-of-the-Wave, the white moon is shining,
>   And we are all pining, sweet sister, for thee.
> Maid-of-the-Wave, would thou wert near us!
>   Come now to cheer us—Oh, hear us! Oh, hear us!

The weeping mother kissed her boys and her baby-girl once again. Then she put on her skin covering and, hastening down the beach, plunged into the sea. Ere long, sounds of joy and laughter were heard far out amongst the billows, and they grew fainter and fainter until they were heard no more. The moon rose high and fair, and shone over the wide solitary ocean, and whither the mermaids had gone no one could tell.

When the crofter returned next morning he found the children fast asleep. He wakened Kenneth, who told him about finding the key and opening the box.

" Where is the key now?" the crofter asked.

" I gave it to Mother," said the boy.

The crofter went towards the box. It was open, and the skin covering was gone. Then he knew what had happened, and sat down and sorrowed because Maid-of-the-Wave had gone.

It is told that the lost mother often returned at night-time to gaze through the cottage windows on her children as they lay asleep. She left trout and salmon for them outside the door. When the boys found the fish they wondered greatly, and their father wept and said: "Your mother is far away, but she has not forgotten you."

"Will Mother return again?" the boys would ask.

"No, Mother will not return," their father would say. "She now dwells in the home of her people, to which you and I can never go."

When the boys grew up they became bold and daring seamen, and no harm ever came to them in storm or darkness, for their mother, Maid-of-the-Wave, followed their ship and protected it from all peril.

A mermaid has power to grant three wishes, for she is one of the fairy folk of ocean and a subject of Queen Beira's.

Once a seaman saw a Maid-of-the-Wave sitting on a rock. He crept towards her unheard and unseen, and seized her in his arms.

"Let me go!" the mermaid cried, "or I shall drag you into the sea."

"I shall not let you go," said the seaman, who was very strong, "until you have granted me three wishes."

"What are your wishes?" asked the mermaid.

"Health, wealth, and prosperity."

"Your wishes are granted," exclaimed the mermaid, who, being then released, plunged into the sea and vanished from sight.

Sometimes a mermaid will give good advice to human beings. There was once a man in Galloway who had skill as a curer of diseases, and it was said that he received some of his knowledge from a mermaid. A beautiful girl named May was ill with consumption. The Galloway herbalist tried in vain to cure her, and as he loved her dearly and wished to marry her, his heart was very sad when he found that his herbs did not do her any good. One evening as he sat sorrowing on the shore, a mermaid raised her head above the waves and sang:

> Would you let bonnie May die in your hand
> And the mugwort [1] flowering in the land?

Then she vanished. The man went at once and gathered the flowers of the mugwort, and made a medicine. This he gave to May, who was soon restored to health.

A mermaid may be offended by anyone who interferes with her, and if she is offended she may do harm.

An old family once lived in a house called Knock-dolion, which stood on the banks of the Water of Girvan in Ayrshire. There was a black stone at

---

[1] Also called "southernwood". It is an aromatic plant allied to "wormwood".

the end of the house, and a mermaid used to come and sit on it, combing her hair and singing for hours on end. The lady of the house could not get her baby to sleep because of the loud singing of the mermaid, so she told her men-servants to break up the stone. This they did, and when the mermaid came on the night that followed she found no stone to sit upon. She at once flew into a rage, and cried to the lady of the house:—

> Ye may think on your cradle—
> I think on my stane;
> There will ne'er be an heir
> To Knockdolian again.

Not long after this the baby died. He was the only child in the house, and when his father and mother died the family became extinct.

Once a Forfarshire landowner nearly lost his life by rushing into a lake towards a mermaid. He thought she was a young lady who had got beyond her depths while bathing. As she struggled in the water she called to him: "Help! help! or I'll drown." When the landowner entered the lake his man-servant followed him and hauled him back. "That wailing woman," the servant said, "is not a human being but a mermaid. If you had touched her, she would have dragged you down and drowned you." As he spoke the sound of laughter came over the lake, and the mermaid was seen swimming away in the dusk.

CHAPTER XIV

Exiles from Fairyland

The Fairy Queen banishes from Fairyland any fairy who disobeys her orders. Then the exile wanders about alone through the land in search of companions. As the queen's subjects shun the banished fairy man or woman, he or she must needs make friends with human beings.

The Goona[1] is the name given to one class of fairy exiles. A Goona is very kindly and harmless, and goes about at night trying to be of service to mankind. He herds the cattle on the hills, and keeps them away from dangerous places. Often he is seen sitting on the edge of a cliff, and when cattle come near he drives them back. In the summer and autumn seasons he watches the cornfields, and if a cow should try to enter one, he seizes it by a horn and leads it to hill pasture. In winter time, when the cattle are kept in byres, the Goona feels very lonely, having no work to do.

Crofters speak kindly of the Goona, and con-

[1] Pronounced Goo'na. Spelled Gunna in Gaelic.

sider themselves lucky when one haunts their
countryside. They tell that he is a little fairy
man with long golden hair that falls down over
his shoulders and back. He is clad in a fox's
skin, and in wintry weather he suffers much from
cold, for that is part of his punishment. The
crofters pity him, and wish that he would come
into a house and sit beside a warm fire, but this
he is forbidden to do. If a crofter were to offer
a Goona any clothing the little lonely fellow would
have to go away and he could never return again.
The only food the exiled fairy can get are scraps
and bones flung away by human beings. There
are songs about the Goona. One tells:

> He will watch the long weird night,
> When the stars will shake with fright,
> Or the ghostly moon leaps bright
> > O'er the ben like Beltane fire.
> If my kine should seek the corn
> He will turn them by the horn,
> And I'll find them all at morn
> > Lowing sweet beside the byre.

Only those who have "second sight"—that is,
the power to see supernatural beings and future
events—can behold a Goona. So the song tells:

> Donald Ban has second sight,
> And he'll moan the Goona's plight
> When the frosts are flickering white,
> > And the kine are housed till day;

For he 'll see him perched alone
On a chilly old grey stone,
Nibbling, nibbling at a bone
    That we 've maybe thrown away.

He 's so hungry, he 's so thin,
If he 'd come we 'd let him in;
For a rag of fox's skin
    Is the only thing he 'll wear.
He 'll be chittering in the cold
As he hovers round the fold,
With his locks of glimmering gold
    Twined about his shoulders bare.

Another exiled fairy is called " The Little Old
Man of the Barn ". He lives to a great age—
some say until he is over two hundred years old
—but he remains strong and active although his
back is bent and his long grey beard reaches to
his ankles. He wears grey clothing, and the
buttons of his coat are of silver. On his high
peaked cap there is a white owl's feather. The
face of the little old man is covered with wrinkles,
but his eyes are bright and kindly. He is always
in a hurry, and hobbles about, leaning on his staff,
but he walks so quickly that the strongest man
can hardly keep up with him. When he begins
to work he works very hard and very quickly.
He will not hold a conversation with anyone once
he begins to perform a task. If a man who has
second sight should address him, saying: " How
are you, old man?" he will answer: " I'm busy,

busy, busy." If he should be asked: "What are you doing?" he will give the same answer, repeating it over and over again. It is no use trying to chat with the little old man.

There was once an old crofter whose name was Callum. He had seven strong sons, but one by one they left him to serve as keepers of the deer. Callum was left to do all the work on the croft. He had to cut the corn and thresh it afterwards, and had it not been for the assistance given him by the " Little Old Man of the Barn ", he would never have been able to get the threshing done.

Each night the fairy man entered the barn and worked very hard. The following verses are from a song about Callum:—

When all the big lads will be hunting the deer,
And no one for helping old Callum comes near,
Oh, who will be busy at threshing his corn?
Who will come in the night and be going at morn?—
   The Little Old Man of the Barn.
   Yon Little Old Man—
   So tight and so braw, he will bundle the straw,
   The Little Old Man of the Barn.

When the peat will turn grey, and the shadows fall deep,
And weary old Callum is snoring asleep;
When yon plant by the door will keep fairies away,
And the horseshoe sets witches a-wandering till day,
   The Little Old Man of the Barn,
   Yon Little Old Man
   Will thrash with no light in the mouth of the night—
   The Little Old Man of the Barn.

There was once a fairy exile who lived in a wood in Gairloch, Ross-shire. He was called Gillie Dhu, which means "dark servant", because he had dark hair and dark eyes. He wore a green garment made of moss and the leaves of trees. Nobody feared him, for he never did any harm.

Once a little girl, whose name was Jessie Macrae, was wandering in the wood and lost her way. It was in summer time, and the air was warm. When evening came on Jessie began to grow afraid, but although she hastened her steps she could not find her way out of the wood. At length, weary and footsore, she sat down below a fir tree and began to weep. A voice spoke to her suddenly from behind, saying: "Why are you crying, little girl?"

Jessie looked round and saw the Gillie Dhu. He had hair black as the wing of a raven, eyes brown as hazel-nuts in September, and his mouth was large; he had a hundred teeth, which were as small as herring bones. The Gillie Dhu was smiling: his cream-yellow cheeks had merry dimples, and his eyes were soft and kindly. Had Jessie seen him at a distance, with his clothing of moss and leaves, she would have run away in terror, but as he seemed so kindly and friendly she did not feel the least afraid.

"Why are you crying, little girl?" the Gillie

JESSIE MACRAE AND THE GILLIE DHU

From a drawing by John Duncan, A.R.S.A.

asked again. "Your tear-drops are falling like dew on the little blue flowers at your feet."

"I have lost my way," said Jessie in a low voice, "and the night is coming on."

Said the Gillie: "Do not cry, little girl; I shall lead you through the wood. I know every path—the rabbit's path, the hare's path, the fox's path, the goat's path, the path of the deer, and the path of men."

"Oh, thank you, thank you!" Jessie said. She looked the fairy up and down, and wondered to see his strange clothing.

"Where do you dwell, little girl?" asked Gillie Dhu.

Jessie told him, and he said: "You have been walking every way but the right way. Follow me, and you'll reach home before the little stars come out to peer at me through the trees."

The Gillie turned round about, and began to trip lightly in front of the girl. He went so fast that she feared she would lose sight of him, but he turned round again and again, and when he found she was far behind, he danced a pretty dance until she came up to him. Then he scampered on as before.

At length Jessie reached the edge of the wood, and saw her home beside the loch. The Gillie bade her good-bye, and said: "Have I not led you well? Do not forget me. I am the Gillie

Dhu, and I love little girls and little boys. If ever you get lost in the wood again, I shall come to your aid. Good-bye, little girl, good-bye."

He laughed merrily, and then trotted away and was soon lost to sight among the trees.

There was once a fairy exile who was a dummy. The Fairy Queen had punished him for some offence by taking away his powers of speech and hearing, and forbade any other fairy to go near him. He wore a bright red jacket and green breeches, and from beneath his little red cap his long curling hair, which was yellow as broom, dropped down on his shoulders. The dummy had cheeks red as rowan berries and laughing blue eyes, and he was always smiling. It made one happy to look at him. He was always so contented and pleased and playful, although he was deaf and dumb, that he put everyone who met him in good humour.

For a long time the fairy dummy lived all alone beneath a great heap of stones, called the Grey Cairn, on a lonely moor in the Black Isle, in Ross-shire. This cairn is in a fir wood which skirts the highway.

When a cart came along the highway the fairy dummy used to steal out from behind a big grey stone, smiling and smiling. Then he would jump on the axle of a wheel, and whirl round and round; and the faster the cart would go the better he would be pleased. He would drop off the axle at the edge of the wood, but he never forgot to turn round and smile to the driver as he ran away.

The people liked to see the little fairy dummy whirling round and round on the cart-wheel, because they believed he always brought them luck.

One day a farmer and his wife were going to the Fair of St. Norman at Cromarty to sell their butter and eggs, but when they reached the big grey stone the Little Red Dummy did not come in sight.

The farmer, who was ill-tempered that day, wanted to go on without giving the little fellow a whirl on the cart-wheel, but his wife said: "No, no; if you will not wait for him, I'll get down and walk home; for we would have no luck at the Fair if we missed the bonnie wee red man."

The woman was looking through the trees, and suddenly she began to laugh.

"Look, Sandy dear, look!" she cried, "there comes the Little Red Dummy—the bonnie wee man—oh, the dear little fairy!"

The farmer was frowning and ill-tempered, but when he looked round he began to smile, for the little red fairy was smiling so sweetly to him. He whipped up his mare, and cried over his shoulder to his wife: "Is he on the wheel yet, Kirsty dear; is he on the wheel?"

"Yes, yes, Sandy dear," Kirsty answered, "he's on now.   Go faster, Sandy—the faster you go the better he'll be pleased."

The farmer cried to the mare: "Gee-up, Jenny, gee-up, my lass!" and the old mare went trotting along the highway, while the little red fairy sat on the axle, whirling round and round with the wheel, and smiling and smiling all the time.

When he dropped off at the edge of the wood, his bright yellow hair was streaming over his laughing eyes, and his cheeks were redder than hazel-berries.   The fairy smiled to Sandy and smiled to Kirsty, looking over his shoulder as he ran away.

"The dear wee man!" cried the farmer's wife.

"The happy little chap," cried the farmer.

They both looked back to see the glint of the fairy's red jacket as he ran merrily through the trees.   They both felt very happy, and they were happier still when they were on their way homeward, because they had secured good prices for their butter and eggs at the Fair.

There was a miller who had a mill with a water-wheel in a woody dell not far from the Grey Cairn. The little fairy dummy was fond of him, because he got many a fine whirl on the mill-wheel. Every morning and every evening the miller left a little cog of oatmeal porridge on the window-sill for the wee red man.   Sometimes, when he was busy tying the bags of meal, the fairy would look in at the door and smile and smile, until the miller felt so happy that he forgot he was old, and began to whistle or sing like a young lad on a bright May morning.

When the miller was getting frail, the little red fairy used to help him at his work. Every now and then he would run out to whirl round the mill-wheel, and he would come back with the spray clinging to his hair like dew-drops on whin blossom.

CHAPTER XV

Friends and Foes of Man

In ancient days the dog was looked upon as man's best friend, and the enemy of all supernatural beings: fairies, giants, hags, and monsters of the sea and the Underworld. When the seasons changed on the four "quarter days" of the year, and the whole world, as the folks believed, was thrown into confusion, the fairies and other spirits broke loose and went about plundering houses and barns and stealing children. At such times the dogs were watchful and active, and howled warning when they saw any of the supernatural creatures. They even attacked the fairies, and sometimes after such fights they returned home with all the hair scraped off their bodies.

A story is still current in Edinburgh about a piper and his dog, and their meeting with a monster of the Underworld. This monster haunted an underground passage, which is said to run from Edinburgh Castle to Holyrood Palace, and was called Great-Hand, for no one ever saw aught of it except its gigantic grisly hand with nails like an eagle's claw.

In days of long ago the underground passage
was used by soldiers when the enemies of the
King of Scotland invaded the kingdom and laid
siege to Edinburgh Castle, his chief stronghold.
The soldiers could leave the castle and fall upon
the besiegers from behind, and through it reinforce-
ments could be sent to the castle. When, however,
the spirit called Great-Hand began to haunt the
tunnel, it could not be used any longer, for every
man who entered it perished in the darkness.

The piper was a brave man, and he resolved
to explore the tunnel with his dog. " I shall play
my bagpipe all the way through," he said to his
friends, "and you can follow the sound of the
piping above the ground."

There is a cave below the castle which leads
to the tunnel, and the piper entered it one morning, playing a merry tune. His faithful dog followed him. The people heard the sound of the
bagpipe as they walked down High Street, listening intently, but when they reached the spot which
is called the " Heart of Midlothian " the piping
stopped abruptly, as if the pipes had been torn suddenly from the piper's hands. The piper was never
seen again, but his dog, without a hair on its body,
came running out of the cave below the castle.

There are other strange passages below hills,
and even below the sea, about which stories have
been told. The longest of these is one that is

supposed to stretch from a cave in Oban to another
cave in the Island of Mull.   A Gaelic legend tells
that a piper once entered the cave at Oban to
explore the tunnel, but was never seen again.
His dog returned with every hair torn from its
body, and died soon afterwards.

It is said that most of these passages have been
made by fairies for the monster with the gigantic
grisly Hand, and there are two stories about men
who once caught glimpses of the Hand inside
caves, and yet managed to escape from it.

The first story is about an underground passage,
over three miles long, that is said to connect the
Dropping Cave, near Cromarty, with another
cave in the fairy-haunted dell of Eathie, which is
situated beside Navity Moor, where in ancient
times the Earth Goddess was worshipped within
a grove.   It is told that when fires are lit in one
of the caves the smoke comes out of the other.

The Dropping Cave is so called because drops
of water are constantly falling from its ceiling,
which bristles with long tapering stalactites that
look like icicles.   There are lots of strange stories
about this cave.   Fishermen have told that they
have seen blue lights hovering near it in the
darkness, and also that often, on moonlight nights,
a mermaid sits on a rock below it, combing her
long yellow hair with her fingers and singing a
low sad song.

Once upon a time a little old man, with a pale wrinkled face and long grey beard, was seen sitting near the cave, gazing over the sea. He did not move for three days. People crept along the lonely shore to watch him from a distance, and fishermen, passing in their boats, stared at him with wondering eyes. No one dared to go near him except a half-witted lad, who first walked round the little old man, and then spoke, saying: "Why are you sitting here? Are you not tired yet?"

The little old man made no answer, but shivered all over. Terrified by his appearance, the lad turned at once and fled homeward, crying: "He is shivering now, he is shivering now."

On the evening of the third day the little old man disappeared. Soon afterwards a terrible storm broke out. It raged fiercely for several days, and, when it was over, the shores were strewn with wreckage and the bodies of drowned sailors. The people believed that the little old man was one of the inhabitants of the Underworld, and some have declared he was no other than Thomas the Rhymer.

A Cromarty man, named William Millar, who lived over a hundred years ago, is said to have entered the Dropping Cave and explored part of the underground passage. When he returned he told that he had caught a glimpse of the great Hand.

Before he entered the cave, Millar sewed sprigs of rowan and witch hazel in the hem of his vest. Into one of his pockets he put a Bible, and in his right hand he held a staff of blackthorn which he had cut on a calm night when the moon was full, and had dressed without using anything made of iron.   With the aid of these charms he hoped to be able to protect himself against the spirits of the Under-world.

Having lit a torch, Millar climbed up to the mouth of the dark wet cave, and entered it just as the sun was beginning to rise.   He walked forward until the passage became so low and narrow that he had to crawl on his hands and knees.   He crawled for some distance until the cave began to widen, and at length he found himself in a big underground chamber which was full of blue mist.   A small and beautiful rainbow appeared round his flaming torch.   For a time he stood gazing around him and above.   The roof seemed to be very high, and the rocky walls were rough and bare.   He walked onward, and as he did so the sound of his footsteps awoke many echoes loud and faint.   It seemed as if a hundred people were walking through the cave.

Suddenly Millar heard a curious humming noise. He stopped to listen, and when he did so the humming grew louder.   He peered through the blue mist for a time, fearing to advance farther

into the depths of that fearsome place. Then a
fierce gust of wind blew in his face. The flames
of the torch were swept backward, flickered, and
went out. Just as this happened, Millar caught
a glimpse of many dim forms flitting round about
him. A cry of fear came from his lips, and he
turned to run away, but stumbled over a stone,
fell heavily, and became unconscious.

How long he lay there he never could tell.
When he woke, the chamber was no longer dark,
for a red light shone through it. The humming
noise had grown very loud, and seemed to be the
noise of falling water. Thinking he was not far
from the waterfalls of Eathie burn, he rose up and
hastened forward. The passage grew narrow,
and led to another large chamber, where he saw
a great fire of fir logs burning fiercely, and a
waterfall dashing over a rock into a deep pool
beneath. In front of the pool was a big stone
chest. The floor of the rocky chamber was strewn
with human bones.

Millar crept forward cautiously until he saw a
big iron mace, red with rust and blood, lying at
one end of the stone chest, and a horn dangling on
a chain which came down from the rocky ceiling.

He gazed at the horn for a minute; then he
grasped it in his hands and blew a single blast
which awoke a hundred echoes.

No sooner did he do so than the waters ceased

to fall. Millar was astonished, and thought he would blow the horn once again to see what would happen. But when he leaned forward to grasp it, he saw the lid of the stone chest rising slowly. He stepped back at once, for a sudden fear struck him, and he began to tremble like an aspen leaf.

The lid rose and rose, and suddenly fell backward with a crash. Then out of the chest came a gigantic grisly Hand which grasped the big rusty mace. Millar shrieked and fled out of the rocky chamber. A fierce yell broke out behind him, and, turning round, he saw the Hand throwing down the mace, the lid of the chest rising, and the waterfall beginning to pour again over the rocks into the deep pool.

With hasty steps he ran into the chamber in which he had lain in a swoon, and having found his torch, lit it again, and crept forward until he reached the narrow passage through which he had crawled. When at length he got out of the Dropping Cave, he found that the sun was setting over the western hills. He vowed never again to attempt to explore the underground passage to Eathie.

Another cave story is told about a west-coast man named MacFadyen, who had a wonderful black dog which he had got from a fairy. This animal was very lazy, and used to sleep a great

deal, and eat huge quantities of food. Mac-
Fadyen's wife hated it, and often said to her
husband: "Your black dog is quite useless; it
eats much food, and never does anything to help
you. I think it should be drowned."

Mac Fadyen would not drown it, however.
"Leave it alone," he would say; "the dog will
have its day."

One morning many of the villagers went out to
hunt the wild deer on the mountains. They roused
a great fleet-footed stag which ran towards the
village. All the dogs were behind it in full chase,
except Mac Fadyen's dog, which lay sleeping in
the sunshine at the corner of his house. The
stag was heading for the loch, over which it could
swim, and so escape from its pursuers, but it had
first to pass Mac Fadyen's dog. Someone said:
"Now the dog's great day has come at last."

The hunters shouted and their dogs bayed
aloud. Mac Fadyen's dog was awakened by the
tumult, and, rising up, stretched itself and looked
round about. It saw the great stag, but never
moved to attack. Instead, it just lay down again
and closed its eyes, and the stag entered the water
and swam across the loch.

"Kill that lazy dog of yours, Mac Fadyen," the
hunters cried out; "it is of no use."

Said Mac Fadyen: "Leave the dog alone; the
dog will have its day."

One morning MacFadyen and other two men went out to fish round the shores of a lonely island.   When the boat was launched the dog walked down the beach, and leaping into it, stretched itself at MacFadyen's feet and went to sleep.

"We do not require a dog when we go fishing," one of the men said.   "Put your dog ashore, MacFadyen."

Said MacFadyen: "Leave the dog alone; the dog will have its day."

The men fished round the island all day, and when evening was coming on they landed and went to a cave.   They lit a fire there and cooked some fish.   MacFadyen's dog ate as much fish as did the three men together.

Night came on, and the men lay down to sleep. MacFadyen had his dog beside him, and in the middle of the night the dog woke him with its growling.   MacFadyen sat up.   The fire was burning low, and in the silence he heard a dripping sound.   He threw some dry twigs on the fire, and when the flames from them lit up the cave, he saw that both his friends were dead.   The dripping he heard was the dripping of their blood flowing over the flat stones.   The light went out, and MacFadyen sat trembling in the darkness while the dog kept growling angrily.   Then MacFadyen heard a rustling sound, and saw, passing over the embers of the low fire, a great grisly Hand. It was feeling round about the cave for something, and MacFadyen shrank back to escape from it. Suddenly his dog leapt up and attacked the giant Hand. A fierce struggle followed. The Hand tried to grasp the dog, and the dog tried to tear the Hand to pieces. For several minutes the fight was waged with fury, and then the Hand was withdrawn. The dog followed it, and scampered out of the cave, and MacFadyen, trembling in the darkness, heard a great stamping overhead.

He waited until the dawn began to break. Then he rose and left the cave, and ran down the beach. With a great effort he launched the boat, and, leaping into it, began to row away from the haunted island.

He had not rowed a hundred yards when he saw two bright lights following him in the dusk of the dawn. Terrified by the lights, he bent himself to the oars and rowed faster and faster. The boat went quickly through the water, but the lights came quickly after him. In the growing brightness of early morning, MacFadyen saw at length that the lights he dreaded were the flaming eyes of his dog, which was swimming from the island and endeavouring to reach the boat. The fury of the fight had roused all the slumbering energy of the dog, and MacFadyen was afraid

of it. He did not wait for it, but kept on row-
ing until the dog became exhausted and, sinking
below the waves, was drowned.

"The dog has had its day," said MacFadyen.
"It saved my life."

There are many Gaelic stories about faithful
dogs, and some examples of these are as follows.

A man named Colin Cameron had once a great
fleet-footed greyhound. He went out to hunt
with it on a September morning, and lost his way
among the mountains. Night came on, and he
allowed the dog to go ahead and followed it. In
time he came to a lonely shieling on a hill-side,
and saw a light issuing from it. The door was
open, and he looked in. He saw an old woman
clad in green sitting on the floor. She looked up
and spoke, saying: "Are you not coming in,
Colin Cameron?"

Colin suspected that the woman was an evil
spirit, and answered: "Not just now."

"You have lost your way," she said.

"Perhaps I shall find it ere long," he told her.

"If you do not come in," she said next, "I had
better go with you and show you the way to your
house."

"Do not trouble yourself," he answered; "I
shall find my way myself."

Having spoken thus, Colin turned and ran
down the hill-side. Soon he found that his dog

was not following him, and he stopped to call it. As he did so, the sound of a fierce struggle fell on his ears, and he began to run again. He ran a great distance. Then the moon rose up, and he found himself in a glen he knew, and turned his face homewards. He reached his own house in safety, and soon after he entered it his dog came in. The animal had not a hair left on its body except on its ears. It was panting with exhaustion and pain. Lying down at Colin's feet, it licked his hand, and then fell over on its right side and died.

Colin realized at once what had happened. His faithful greyhound had waited behind at the shieling to prevent the green woman from following him.

Another story is told about three men who once crossed a lonely moor in the night-time. They had a dog with them, and when they were half-way on their journey it began to run round and round them in ever-widening circles. At length the men heard the sound of fairy music, and one said to another: "The wee folk are dancing and making merry somewhere near us."

They hastened on their way, fearing to meet the fairies. At length the sound of the dog howling and barking mingled with the music. Suddenly the music stopped abruptly, and they heard the trampling of many feet on the dark moor.   They ran as fast as they were able until the sounds died away in the distance, and they reached in safety the house to which they were going.   Early next morning the dog made its appearance.   All the hair on its body had been scraped off as if with long nails, and soon after it entered the house it lay down and died.

A man named Malcolm Mac Phee was once walking along a lonely rocky beach in Islay when a mermaid seized him.   She thrust him into a cave, and there kept him a prisoner.

Now Mac Phee had a big black dog, and his wife sent it out to search for its master.   The wise animal at once ran towards the cave on the beach, where it found Mac Phee.   No sooner did it arrive, however, than the mermaid rose out of the sea to prevent her prisoner escaping.   The dog growled fiercely when it saw her, and she tried to drive it away.

Said Mac Phee: "You had better let me go, or my dog will attack you."

The mermaid laughed, and answered: "I shall keep you here until you die."

No sooner did she say that than the dog sprang at her.   A fierce struggle took place, and the mermaid tried to escape by leaping back into the sea.   The dog followed her, and fought until it killed the mermaid, but was itself so severely wounded that it was drowned before it reached the shore. MacPhee hastened homeward, lamenting the loss of his faithful dog.

It is told that dogs can see the spirit messenger of death coming nigh in the darkness. When they catch sight of it they begin to howl. People who hear dogs howling at night fear that someone they know will meet with a fatal accident or die suddenly while asleep.

The Banshee is dreaded by dogs. She is a fairy woman who washes white sheets in a ford by night when someone near at hand is about to die. It is said she has the power to appear during day-time in the form of a black dog, or a raven, or a hoodie-crow.

The following is a Highland poem about the Banshee, who is supposed to sing a mournful song while she washes the death-clothes of one who is doomed to meet with a sudden and unexpected death:—

> Knee-deep she waded in the pool—
>   The Banshee robed in green—
> Singing her song the whole night long,
>   She washed the linen clean;
> The linen that must wrap the dead
>   She beetled on a stone;
> She washed with dripping hands, blood-red,
>   Low singing all alone:
>
>> *The Banshee I with second sight,*
>> *Singing in the cold starlight;*
>> *I wash the death-clothes pure and white,*
>> *For Fergus More must die to-night.*

'T was Fergus More rode o'er the hill,
  Come back from foreign wars;
His horse's feet were clattering sweet
  Below the pitiless stars;
And in his heart he would repeat:
  "O never again I 'll roam;
All weary is the going forth,
  But sweet the coming home."

     The Banshee I with second sight,
     Singing in the cold starlight;
     I wash the death-clothes pure and white,
     For Fergus More must die to-night.

He saw the blaze upon his heart
  Bright-gleaming down the glen;
O, he was fain for home again!—
  He 'd parted with his men.
"'T is many a weary day," he 'd sigh,
  "Since I did leave her side;
I 'll never more leave Scotland's shore
  And Una Ban, my bride."

     The Banshee I with second sight,
     Singing in the cold starlight;
     I wash the death-clothes pure and white,
     For Fergus More must die to-night.

With thought of Una's tender love
  Soft tears his eyes did blind,
When up there crept and swiftly leapt
  A man who stabbed behind.
"'T is you," he cried, "who stole my bride.
  This night shall be your last." . . .
As Fergus fell, the warm, red tide
  Of life came ebbing fast.

     The Banshee I with second sight,
     Singing in the cold starlight;
     I wash the death-clothes pure and white,
     For Fergus More must die to-night.

CHAPTER XVI

The Land of Green Mountains

Ronald Booe[1] had rebelled against his chief but was defeated in battle. Then all his followers deserted him, and he found that he would have to flee from his native land. It chanced that he had heard tell of the wonderful Land of Green Mountains nigh to the world's end, in which there were great herds of wild animals, while fish could be caught in plenty round its shores and in its rivers. He made up his mind to go there and live happily and at ease. As he had no children, it was not difficult for him and his wife to depart in secret.

One fair morning they launched a boat and set sail. Ronald's heart was made glad when he found himself far out on the wide blue sea. The broad grey sail swallowed the wind, and the creaking of the ropes was like sweet music in his ears. Ronald loved the shrill cry of the breeze that blew so steadily and tossed the sparkling brine-spray through the air in bright sunshine.

[1] Pronounced Boo'e. The name means "Yellow-haired Ronald".

The whisperings and mutterings of the waves that went past the boat seemed to repeat over and over again the old song of the sea:

> Sweet to me, Oh, sweet to me
> Is a life at sea, is a life at sea!

When the shore melted from sight Ronald's wife felt very lonely and sad. "I wish," she said, "I could see the high brown hills of my own country."

Said Ronald: "There is no voyage so long that it will not come to an end. Speak not of brown hills, for we are voyaging to the wonderful Land of Green Mountains.

They sailed on and on for six days and six nights, and while the one slept the other sat at the helm. On the morning of the seventh day a storm arose. "Alas," the woman cried, "the boat will be dashed to pieces and we shall perish!"

Said Ronald: "Have no fear, Morag, daughter of Donald; am I not a skilled seaman? In storm and calm I am a king of the sea. My boat bounds over the waves like a spray-bright bird, and there is joy in my heart even in the midst of danger."

The sky darkened, and the wind blew fiercer and louder, while the bounding waves gaped and bellowed liked angry monsters seeking for their prey. Crouching low, the woman moaned and wept with fear, until at length Ronald called to her, saying: "I see land ahead."

His wife rose up and gazed towards the horizon. With glad eyes she saw before her the wonderful Land of Green Mountains. Thereupon she dried her tears and smiled.

It was not until late evening, however, that the boat drew nigh to the shore. Ronald tried to steer towards a safe landing-place, but, while yet some distance from it, the boat struck a hidden rock and began to sink. Ronald grasped an oar with one hand and his wife with the other, and leapt into the raging sea. He was a strong swimmer, and, after a hard struggle, he managed to reach shallow water, and then wade ashore.

There was a cave near where he landed, and he carried his wife to it. Then he gathered dry sticks and withered grass and lit a fire by using flint and steel. Soon the flames were leaping high, and Ronald and his wife were able to dry their clothes. Then they lay down to sleep, and, although the sea roared all night long, they slept soundly.

Next morning Ronald found on the beach a keg of salt herring, a keg of meal, and a pot which had been washed ashore from the boat. His wife cooked the herring, and baked oatmeal cakes, and after the two had eaten of these they felt quite happy.

A day or two went past, and then their store
of food ran short.   Ronald had no weapons with
which to hunt game, and no hooks with which
to catch fish, so he said to his wife: " I will go
inland and explore this strange Land of Green
Mountains.   Do not be anxious or afraid."

"You may lose your way," his wife said.

"There is no fear of that," Ronald answered.
" I'll put marks on the trees as I go through
forests, and set up stones on the plains I cross."

Early next morning Ronald set out on his
journey.   As he passed through the wood he
chipped the bark off trees, and on the plain he
set up stones.   After leaving the wood, he saw
a high green mountain, and walked towards it.
"When I reach the top," he said to himself, " I
shall get a better view of this strange land."

The sun was beginning to set when he found
himself on the crest of the green mountain.   He
looked round about and could see many other
green mountains but there was no sign of human
beings, and his heart grew very sad.   Although
he was very tired and very hungry he did not
despair however.   " I'll go down the other side
of this green mountain," he said to himself, "and
perhaps I shall have better luck."

He began to descend in the dusk, and before
long he saw a light.   It came from a little house
among trees on the lower slope of the mountain,

and he walked towards it. Darkness was coming on when he reached the house, and as the door was open he walked in.

To his surprise he found no one inside. A bright fire was burning, and near it stood a table and two chairs. The table was covered with a green cloth, and on it were two dishes of food.

" I am very hungry," said Ronald, "and must eat. I hope I shall not be found fault with for helping myself."

He sat down and ate all the food that was on one of the plates. Then he felt happy and con- tented. Suddenly he heard the sound of footsteps, and, looking up, he saw an old grey-bearded man entering the house.

" Well, stranger," this man said, "who are you, and where have you come from?"

Ronald said: " My boat was wrecked on the shore. I have been wandering about all day searching for food, and found naught until I came here. I hope you are not angry with me for eating without leave."

Said the old man: " You are welcome to my food. You can stay here to-night. I live all alone, and always keep enough food to give to any visitor who may come hither as you have done."

Ronald thanked the old man for his kindness, and said: " I shall tell you all about myself in the hope that you may help me with good advice."

The old man sat down, and, as he ate his meal, Ronald told the story of his life. When he had finished the other asked: "Have you any children?"

"No," Ronald said, "I have no children."

"That is a pity," the old man sighed.

Next morning the old man wakened Ronald and said: "Breakfast is ready. It is time you were on your way back to the cave, for your wife is anxious and afraid."

When Ronald had eaten an excellent breakfast he said: "I wish I had food to carry to my wife."

Said the old man: "What will you give me for this green table-cloth? When you want food all you have to do is to shake it three times and lay it down. As soon as you lay it down you will get all the food you need."

Ronald was surprised to hear this. He looked at the green cloth, and, sighing, made answer: "Alas! I am very poor, having lost everything I possessed. I am not able to offer you anything for the green cloth."

Said the old man: "Will you promise to give me your eldest son for it?"

Having no son, Ronald promised readily.

"Very well," the old man said; "come back

here in seven years, and bring your son with you."

Ronald took the cloth, and bade good-bye to the old man. He climbed the green mountain and went down the other side of it. Then he crossed the plain, past the stones he had set up, and walked through the wood, guiding himself by the marks he had made on the trees. He had no difficulty in finding his way. The sun was beginning to set as he reached the shore and hastened towards the cave, where he found his wife sitting beside the fire moaning and weeping. She feared that her husband had been devoured by wild beasts.

"Here I am, Morag, daughter of Donald," he said as he entered the cave.

His wife rose to her feet and kissed him joyfully.

"I have brought food for you," said Ronald.

As he spoke he shook the green cloth three times, and laid it on the floor of the cave beside the fire. As soon as he did that, two dishes of hot, steaming food appeared before their wondering eyes.

They sat down and ate the food. "Where did you find this wonderful green cloth?" asked Morag.

"It was given to me by an old grey-bearded man," Ronald told her. "Are we not in luck now? We shall never want for food as long as we live."

Several days went past. Then Ronald and his wife thought they would go inland and explore the country. They felt lonely, and wished to find out where the people who inhabited it had their dwellings.

For six days they travelled inland, and on the morning of the seventh day they reached a village. The people were kindly and hospitable and invited them to stay. Ronald thought he might as well do so, and next morning began to build a house. He got every assistance from the villagers, and soon had a home of his own among his newly-found friends. Before the year was out a baby boy was born, and Ronald and Morag's hearts were filled with joy. They called the baby Ian.

Years went past, and Ian grew up to be a handsome boy with curly golden hair, sea-grey eyes, and red cheeks. Everyone in the village loved him, and he was very dear to his father and mother.

Ronald Booe remembered the promise he had made to the grey old man, but he never told Morag his wife about it until the seventh year was nearly at an end. Then one day he said: "On the morrow I must go to the mountain house with Ian, because I promised the grey old man, when I was given the green cloth, to do so."

Morag cried: "Alas! alas!" and began to moan

and weep. "It was foolish and wicked of you," she said, "to make such a promise."

Said Ronald: "What can I do? My heart bleeds to part with our boy, but I must go, and he must go with me."

Next morning he bade his wife good-bye, and she kissed Ian and wept over him. Father and son then set out on their journey, and in time they reached the dwelling of the grey old man, who spoke, saying: "So you have come, as you said you would."

"Yes," Ronald answered sadly, "I have come."

"Do you find it hard to part with your boy?"

"Indeed, I do. My wife is heart-broken."

Said the grey old man: "You can take him home again if you promise me to come back when another seven years have gone past."

Ronald thanked the grey old man, and, having promised, he returned home with Ian. His wife welcomed him with smiling face and bright eyes, and kissed her child, saying: "If you had stayed away from me I should have died with sorrow."

Ian grew and grew, and when he was twelve years old he was nearly as tall as his father and nearly as strong. He had great skill as a hunter and as a fisherman, and could work in the fields like a man.

When the second term of seven years was drawing to a close his father grew sadder and sadder, and one day he said to his wife: "On the morrow I must go to the mountain house with Ian."

"Alas! alas!" cried his wife; "I cannot live without him."

Said Ronald: "You cannot have your son beside you always. To every youth comes the day when he must leave his parents."

"Wait for a few years," pleaded Morag. "I have not long to live, and I would fain have him beside me until I die."

Said Ronald: "It cannot be as you wish."

"Perhaps," his wife sighed, "the grey old man will send him back for another seven years."

Said Ronald: "He may, and he may not."

Next morning father and son set out on foot towards the mountain house, and when they reached it the grey old man said: "So you have come as you promised. It is well. Do you find it hard to part with the lad?"

Said Ronald: "Indeed, I do. I find it harder now than I did seven years ago."

"Has the boy been well taught?" asked the old man.

Said Ronald: "He can fish, he can shoot, he can work in the fields. I have trained him myself."

"You have trained his body, but I will train his mind," the grey old man told Ronald. "Knowledge is better than strength. You will be proud of Ian some day."

The boy's father was stricken with sorrow when he found that the old man intended to keep Ian. He returned home alone. Morag wept bitterly when he entered the house, and all Ronald could say to comfort her was: "The grey old man promised that we should be proud of Ian some day."

Morag refused to be comforted, for she knew well that many years must pass before she would see her son again.

The grey old man was like a father to Ian. He spent six years in teaching the lad, and on the seventh he said: "Now you have passed your twentieth year. You are strong, and you are well educated. It is time you began to work for yourself. Before you go to look for a situation, however, I shall take you on a long journey, so that you may meet friends who may help you in time of need. It is better to make friends than to make enemies."

Said Ian: "I am ready to do as you advise me."

"Well spoken!" the old man exclaimed. "You have learned to obey. He who learns how to obey will rise to command. Come with me to the mountain-top. Behind the door hangs a silver bridle. Take it with you."

Ian took the bridle. and followed the old man.

On the mountain-top the old man said: "If you will shake the bridle over me I shall become a grey horse. You can then jump on my back, and we shall go forward quickly."

Ian shook the bridle as he was asked to do. The man changed at once into a grey horse, and as soon as Ian mounted, the horse galloped away at a rapid pace. Over hill and over moor went the horse. Nor did it pause until seven hours went past. Then Ian heard the old man's voice, saying: "Dismount and shake the bridle over me."

Ian did as he was ordered, and the grey man at once returned to his own form again. He spoke, saying: "Go and gather red moss, and fill your water-stoup at the well below yonder red rock."

Ian gathered the moss, and filled his water-stoup, and returned to the old man, who said: "Go now to the cave which opens behind the waterfall. Inside it you will find a wounded giant. Dress his wounds with the red moss, and give him three draughts from your water-stoup."

Ian climbed down the side of the waterfall over slippery rocks, and when he entered the cave he saw the wounded giant. He put red moss on the giant's wounds, and bound it round with cords made of dried reeds. Then he gave the sufferer three draughts from his water-stoup. As soon as he did that, the giant sat up and cried out: "I am feeling better now. Ere long I shall be well again."

"Remember me and be my friend," said Ian.

"Your friend I shall be," the giant answered.

Ian then returned to the old man, who asked him at once: "Have you done as I ordered you to do?"

"Yes," Ian answered.

"It is well," the old man told him. "Shake your bridle over me again, and then leap on my back, so that we may go forward quickly."

The old grey man in horse shape went galloping on and on, until a lonely shore was reached. Once more he called: "Shake the bridle over me," and when Ian had done so, the man appeared in his own form and said: "Go down the ebb until you reach a flat brown stone. Behind that stone lies the King of Fish. Lift him up and put him into the sea, for this is a day of misfortune for him, and he is in need of help."

Ian ran down the long dreary sands until he reached the flat brown stone. He found the fish lying gasping and twitching and helpless. Lifting him up, Ian put him into the sea and, as he did so, cried out: "Remember me and be my friend."

The fish answered him, saying: "Your friend I shall be," and then vanished.

Ian returned to the old man and once again changed him into a horse. They went onward together, and ere long reached a bronze castle on a lonely headland overlooking the sea. It was now late evening. The old man said: "Enter the bronze castle, in which dwells a fair lady. You will see rooms full of silver and gold and flashing gems. Look on everything but touch nothing."

Ian went through the castle. He wondered to see so much treasure, but although it seemed to be unprotected, for he did not see the fair lady even, he never touched a single piece of gold or silver. When, however, he was leaving the castle, his eyes fell on a heap of goose feathers. He pulled out a single feather and put it in his pocket, but he did not tell the old man that he had done so.

He mounted the horse, and returned to the grey old man's hut in the gathering darkness, and there the two rested for the night.

Next morning the old man became a horse again, and carried Ian to the capital of the country —a large and beautiful city in the midst of which the king's castle stood on a high rock.

Outside the city wall Ian shook the bridle over the horse, and the old man stood before him and said: "Here we must part. You will go towards the castle, and ask for a situation. The king is in need of a scribe. If he offers to employ you, accept his offer."

Ian then bade good-bye to the old man, who said: "If ever you are in trouble, think of me and I shall come to you."

They parted at the western gate of the city, and Ian walked towards the castle. He told the guards that he was looking for a situation, and after a time they took him before the chief scribe, who said: "I am in need of an assistant. Will you enter the king's service?"

Ian accepted the offer, and next morning began to work. He thought of the goose feather he had taken from the bronze castle, and made a pen of it. When he began to use it, he found that it wrote beautifully, and he was delighted at his own fine penmanship.

The head scribe was greatly surprised at the skill shown by the young man, and grew jealous of him. After a few days he asked Ian for the loan of his pen, and when he tried it he discovered that he could write just as well as Ian.

"This is a magic pen," he said to himself. He then went before the king and told him about it, and the king tried the pen also. "Bring this young scribe before me," he commanded.

Ian was called for, and when he stood before the king he was asked: "Where did you get this magic pen?"

Said Ian: "I found it in a bronze castle."

The king gazed at him in silence for a moment, and then spoke, saying: "There is a beautiful lady in that castle, and she cannot leave it. Bring her here, for I wish her for my bride."

Said Ian: "Alas! O king, I am not able to obey your command. I do not know where the castle is, for I was taken to it at late evening, and returned home in the darkness."

"If you fail to do as I command," said the king, "you shall be put to death."

Ian went to his bedroom, and there wept tears of sorrow. He knew well that this trouble which had befallen him was due to his having disobeyed the old man, who had warned him not to touch anything he saw in the bronze castle. After a time he said aloud: "I wish the grey old man were here now." He heard a noise behind him, and, turning round, he saw the grey old man, who spoke, saying: "What ails you now, Ian?"

"Alas!" cried Ian, "I have done wrong." Then he told the old man how he had taken a goose feather from the bronze castle and made a quill of it, and that the king had discovered his secret, and ordered him to fetch the captive lady from the castle to be the king's bride.

"You should not have touched the feather," the old man said. "It is as wicked to steal a small thing as a great thing. Theft is dishonour-

able, even the theft of trifles. I placed my trust
in you, and you promised to obey me. Because
you have failed in that trust and done this thing,
you now find yourself in trouble."

"Alas!" Ian cried, "I know I have done wrong,
and am sorry for it."

"Let this be a lesson to you," the old man
said. "Because you are sorry for your wrong-
doing, I shall help you once again. Let us go
outside. I have the silver bridle with me. We
shall visit the bronze castle once again."

Ian walked with the old man to a solitary place
outside the city wall. There he shook the bridle,
and his friend became a grey horse. He mounted
and rode away swiftly towards the seaside. Then
he shook the bridle again, and his friend appeared
in human form and spoke to him, saying: "I
have a magic rod. Take it and strike me with it.
When you do so I shall become a ship. Enter
the ship, and it will sail to the harbour below the
bronze castle. Cast anchor there and wait until
the lady looks out of a window and asks you
whence you have come. Say: 'I have come from
a distant land.' Then she will ask: 'What cargo
have you on board?' Say to her: 'I have a cargo
of fine silk.' She will ask you to enter the castle
with samples of the silk, but you will say: 'Would
it not be better if you came on board and examined the rolls of silk?' She will answer: 'Very

well,' and come on board your vessel. Take her down to the cabin, and spread out the rolls of silk you will find lying there."

Ian seized the magic rod and struck the grey old man, who at once became a large and noble ship, afloat beside the rock. Ian got on board the ship, cast off from the rock, and set sail. It had a crew of little men clad in green, with red peaked caps on their heads. The skipper who steered the vessel had a long grey beard and sharp beady eyes. He never spoke a word, but gave orders to the crew by making signs.

The ship sailed swiftly towards the bronze castle on the lonely headland. When the anchor was dropped in the little harbour Ian walked up and down the deck until an upper window in the castle opened, and the beautiful lady looked out and spoke to him, saying: "Where have you come from, my merry sailor man?"

"From a distant land," Ian answered.

"What cargo have you on board?"

"A cargo of fine silk."

"Come up into the castle and bring with you samples of your silk, and I perchance may buy a few rolls from you."

Said Ian: "I have so many kinds of silk that I cannot carry samples to you. Would it not be better if you came on board and examined the cargo, O fair lady?"

"Very well," the lady answered, "I shall do as you suggest."

She came down from the castle and came on board the ship. Ian led her to the cabin, where he spread out before her the rolls of fine silk that he found there.

She examined them all carefully. Then hearing the splashing of waves against the sides of the ship, she ran up the cabin ladder to the deck, and discovered that the vessel was far away from the bronze castle.

"Alas!" she cried, "what is the meaning of this?"

Said Ian: "The king, my master, has ordered me to bring you before him. It is his wish that you should become his queen."

"It is your duty to obey your master, and I do not blame you," the lady said. "But I do not wish to be the king's bride. I should much rather have stayed yet a while in my bronze castle."

As she spoke, she took a bundle of keys from her waist-belt and flung it into the sea. .

"There go my keys!" she told Ian. "No one else can now enter the bronze castle."

The ship sailed back to the place from which it had started, and drew up alongside the rock, and Ian and the lady went ashore. Then Ian waved the magic rod three times. When he did so the ship vanished, and the grey old man appeared by his side and spoke, saying: "Shake the silver bridle over me, so that I may become a horse. Mount me then, and take the lady with you."

Ian shook the bridle, and his friend became a grey horse. He mounted the horse, and the lady mounted behind him. They rode away very swiftly, and when night was coming on they reached the city. Ian shook the bridle again, and the old man appeared by his side, and they bade one another good-bye. Ian led the lady to the castle and brought her to the king. His majesty thanked him for his service, and bade the lady welcome. He called for maidservants to attend to her, and she was taken to her room.

Next morning the king had the lady brought before him, and said: "O fair one, be my bride."

Said the lady: "I shall not be your bride until my bronze castle is brought here and placed beside yours."

"No one can do that but Ian," the king said. Then he called to a servant, saying: "Bring Ian before me."

Ian had returned to his place in the room of the chief scribe, and was busy at his work when he was ordered to appear before his majesty.

He obeyed the summons, and the king said to him: "You must bring the bronze castle from the lonely headland, and have it placed beside my castle."

"Alas!" Ian cried, "I cannot do that."

Said the king: "If you fail to carry out my command you shall be put to death."

Ian went to his room, and paced it up and down for a time, lamenting his fate. Then he cried out: "I wish the grey old man were here."

No sooner had he wished that wish than the grey old man appeared in the room and spoke to him, saying: "What is wrong now, Ian?"

Said Ian: "The king has set me an impossible task. He wants me to have the bronze castle carried here and placed beside his own castle."

"Come with me," the old man said.

Together they went outside the city wall. Ian shook the bridle over his friend, who at once became a grey horse. He mounted the horse, and rode away until he reached the waterfall behind which was the giant's cave. Then he shook the bridle again, and the old man appeared beside him and said: "Enter the cave and speak to the giant whose wounds you helped to heal. Tell him you are in need of his aid, and ask him to carry away the bronze castle and place it beside the castle of your king."

Ian went down the slippery rocks and entered the cave. He found the giant lying asleep on the floor, and walked towards him. As soon as he touched him the giant sat up and asked: "Who are you, and what brings you here, little fellow?"

Ian was at first too terrified to speak, for the giant scowled at him. At length he said: "I am he who dressed your wounds with red moss, and gave you three draughts of the healing water. I am now in need of your help."

Said the giant: "I remember you. I was in great pain, and you gave me healing. What do you wish me to do? Speak and I shall obey, even should you ask me to remove a mountain from its place and cast it into the sea."

Ian laughed aloud, and the giant laughed also, but the giant's laugh was terrible to hear, for it sounded like thunder.

Ian then told the giant that the king wished to have the bronze castle carried from the lonely headland and placed beside his own castle on the rock in the midst of his capital.

Said the giant: "The work shall be done to-night. I shall call all my strong men together. Begone! or it may not go well with you."

Ian thanked the giant, and returned to the grey old man, who said: "We must make haste. There is no time to be lost."

As the grey horse, the old man travelled again swiftly until he reached the capital. Then he bade Ian good-bye.

That night as Ian lay in his bed a great thunder-storm arose and raged furiously. He could not sleep, and lay trembling with fear, for it seemed as if the whole world would be set on fire by the flashes of lightning. When the thunder-storm was at its height there came an earthquake. The rock beneath the castle trembled, and the castle swayed like a ship at sea. Ian was terrified, and he heard the shrieks of those who were even more afraid than he was. At length the storm died down, and he slept.

Next morning when Ian looked through the window of his room he saw the bronze castle beside the king's castle. Then he knew that the thunder-storm had been caused by the giants, and that the earth shook when they set down the castle upon the rock.

The king was greatly pleased, and spoke to the fair lady, saying: "Your bronze castle has been brought hither. Now you will be my queen."

Said the lady: "I cannot marry until I am given the bundle of keys I threw into the sea. The castle door cannot be opened without the keys."

"Ian shall find the keys," the king told her. Then he called for Ian and said to him: "You must find the bundle of keys which this fair lady threw into the sea."

"Alas!" Ian moaned, "you set me a task I cannot fulfil."

"If you do not bring the keys to me," said the king, "you shall be put to death."

Ian turned away and went to his room. He felt sure that his end was near at hand because it did not seem possible that the keys could be found. "I wish the old grey man were here," he cried out.

The old grey man appeared in the room and asked softly: "What does the king ask for now, Ian?"

Said Ian: "He has ordered me to find the bundle of keys which the fair lady threw into the sea."

"Come with me," the grey old man said; "we have a long journey before us."

Ian rode again on the grey horse until he reached the shore where he had found the King of Fish. He then shook the silver bridle and the old man appeared beside him. "Go out on the ebb," he advised Ian, "and call for the King of Fish. When he comes, ask him to search for the keys and bring them to you."

Ian walked down the sands and called for the King of Fish. Three times he called before the fish appeared. Then it rose and asked: "Who are you that you should call upon me?"

Said Ian: "I am the one who found you lying behind the flat brown stone on a day of misfortune when you were in need of help. I lifted you up and put you into the sea, and you promised to remember me and be my friend."

" You speak truly," the fish said. " What is your wish? I am ready to grant it."

Said Ian: " Search for the keys which the fair lady of the bronze castle threw into the sea when I took her away in my ship. When you have found the keys, bring them to me."

The fish vanished and returned soon afterwards.

" Have you found the keys?" he asked.

" I have," answered the fish.

"Give them to me."

" I will give them if you promise one thing."

" What is that?"

" Promise that you will not call for me again."

" I promise," said Ian.

The fish then gave him the keys and vanished at once.

Ian was overjoyed. He ran up the beach towards the old man, who asked: " Have you got the keys?"

" Oh, yes!"

" It is well. Shake the bridle over me and mount."

Ian did so, and rode back to the capital on the back of the grey horse. Having bidden good-bye to his friend, he hastened before the king and handed the keys of the bronze castle to him.

"It is good for you that you found the keys," the king said. "Had you come back without them you would have been put to death."

Ian bowed and turned away, hoping that his troubles were at an end.

The king sent for the lady of the castle and said: "Here are the keys of the bronze castle which my servant found for me."

"He is a brave and noble lad," the lady cried out.

"Now you will marry me," said the king.

"I cannot promise to marry you, O king, until I get a stoup of water from the Healing Well."

Said the king: "I shall order Ian to bring the water without delay."

He sent for Ian, and spoke to him harshly, saying: "Bring hither without delay a stoup of water from the Healing Well."

"Where is that well, O king?" asked Ian.

"I know not," was the answer. "But this I know: if you do not bring the water you will be put to death."

Ian went to his room and wished for the grey old man, who appeared at once and asked: "What ails you now, my poor lad?"

"Alas!" Ian exclaimed, "the king has asked for a stoup of water from the Healing Well, but he does not know where it is."

"We had better make haste and search for it."

Away went Ian again on the back of the grey horse. All day long he rode over hill and dale, through forests and across bogs, over rivers and through lochs, until at length a lonely glen was reached.

"Shake the bridle," called the horse.

Ian shook it, and the old man stood beside him and said: "Strike me with the magic wand and I shall fall down dead."

"I cannot do that," Ian answered at once.

"You must do it. When I am dead three ravens will fly hither. Speak to them saying: 'I shall kill you with my wand unless you take me to the Healing Well.' They will then show you where it is. When you find it, fill two stoups and bring them to this spot. Sprinkle a few drops of the water in my mouth, in my eyes, and in my ears. When you do so, I shall come to life again."

Ian struck the old man with the magic wand and he fell down dead. He lay so still that the young man's heart was filled with sorrow, and he began to weep. "Would that the ravens were here!" he cried out, as he looked round about. To his amaze he saw no sign of the ravens coming.

For over an hour he sat there beside his dead friend, fearing that he would never be able to bring him back to life again.

But at length the ravens came, and Ian stood

up and called out: "I shall kill you with my magic wand if you do not do as I bid you."

"What is your wish?" the ravens asked him in turn.

Said Ian: "Lead me to the Healing Well."

The ravens flew round about above him three times, and then cried out, one after the other: "Follow, follow me."

Ian followed them, and was led to a dark and lonely ravine in which there was a deep cave. The ravens entered the cave, and Ian followed them. Inside he heard the dripping of water, but he saw naught, for the place was very dark.

Said one of the ravens: "Dip your stoups in the pool beside which you stand."

Ian did so, and he lifted them up full of water. Joyfully he hastened out of the cave, and returned to the spot where he had left the old man. He sprinkled water drops in his eyes, in his ears, and in his mouth. When he had done so the old man rose up and said: "Shake the bridle over me."

Ian was soon again on the back of the grey horse. When he returned to the castle it was nigh to midnight. He carried the stoups to his room, and in the morning gave one of them to the king.

The king called for the fair lady, and he handed her the stoup of water and said: "Now you will marry me."

Said the lady: "I cannot marry you until you have fought a duel with Ian. He has done what you cannot do, and is now more powerful than you are."

"You speak truly," the king answered. "This duel must be fought at once."

He called a courtier and told him to hasten to Ian and bid him to make ready for the duel.

Ian was amazed to hear this command, and when he was alone he wished for the grey old man, who appeared and asked at once: "What is wrong now, Ian?"

Ian told him that the king desired to fight a duel.

Said the grey old man: "Wash all your body with the water from the Healing Well. No weapon can wound you when you have done that. I have brought a sword for you."

He handed a small sword to Ian and then vanished.

Ian washed himself with the water from the Healing Well, and then went forth to fight the duel with the king.

Said the fair lady: "He who wins the duel will marry me, and reign over the Land of Green Mountains. Is that not so, O king?"

The king was very vain, and was certain that she expected him to win the duel. He despised Ian with his small sword, and raised his own to strike him.   But although he struck Ian three times he could not wound him.   Then Ian struck once and the king fell dead.

"Hail to the new king!" called the lady of the bronze castle.

All the people called out: "Hail to the king!"

So Ian was crowned king, and he married the fair lady.   His friend, the grey old man, came to the wedding, bringing Ian's father and mother with him.

"Did I not promise you that you would be proud of Ian some day?" said the grey old man to Ronald Booe and Morag, daughter of Donald.

Ere they could make answer, Ian came forward. He embraced and kissed his mother, and shook his father's right hand, and then said: "You shall stay here with me for the rest of your days."

Ian was a wise and good king, and he and his queen were greatly beloved by their people.   Indeed, there was never such a king in the Land of Green Mountains as Ian, son of Ronald Booe and of Morag, daughter of Donald.

A CATALOG OF SELECTED
DOVER BOOKS
IN ALL FIELDS OF INTEREST

A CATALOG OF SELECTED DOVER
BOOKS IN ALL FIELDS OF INTEREST

CONCERNING THE SPIRITUAL IN ART, Wassily Kandinsky. Pioneering work by father of abstract art. Thoughts on color theory, nature of art. Analysis of earlier masters. 12 illustrations. 80pp. of text. 5⅜ x 8½. 23411-8 Pa. $4.95

ANIMALS: 1,419 Copyright-Free Illustrations of Mammals, Birds, Fish, Insects, etc., Jim Harter (ed.). Clear wood engravings present, in extremely lifelike poses, over 1,000 species of animals. One of the most extensive pictorial sourcebooks of its kind. Captions. Index. 284pp. 9 x 12. 23766-4 Pa. $14.95

CELTIC ART: The Methods of Construction, George Bain. Simple geometric techniques for making Celtic interlacements, spirals, Kells-type initials, animals, humans, etc. Over 500 illustrations. 160pp. 9 x 12. (USO) 22923-8 Pa. $9.95

AN ATLAS OF ANATOMY FOR ARTISTS, Fritz Schider. Most thorough reference work on art anatomy in the world. Hundreds of illustrations, including selections from works by Vesalius, Leonardo, Goya, Ingres, Michelangelo, others. 593 illustrations. 192pp. 7⅛ x 10¼. 20241-0 Pa. $9.95

CELTIC HAND STROKE-BY-STROKE (Irish Half-Uncial from "The Book of Kells"): An Arthur Baker Calligraphy Manual, Arthur Baker. Complete guide to creating each letter of the alphabet in distinctive Celtic manner. Covers hand position, strokes, pens, inks, paper, more. Illustrated. 48pp. 8¼ x 11. 24336-2 Pa. $3.95

EASY ORIGAMI, John Montroll. Charming collection of 32 projects (hat, cup, pelican, piano, swan, many more) specially designed for the novice origami hobbyist. Clearly illustrated easy-to-follow instructions insure that even beginning papercrafters will achieve successful results. 48pp. 8¼ x 11. 27298-2 Pa. $3.50

THE COMPLETE BOOK OF BIRDHOUSE CONSTRUCTION FOR WOODWORKERS, Scott D. Campbell. Detailed instructions, illustrations, tables. Also data on bird habitat and instinct patterns. Bibliography. 3 tables. 63 illustrations in 15 figures. 48pp. 5¼ x 8½. 24407-5 Pa. $2.50

BLOOMINGDALE'S ILLUSTRATED 1886 CATALOG: Fashions, Dry Goods and Housewares, Bloomingdale Brothers. Famed merchants' extremely rare catalog depicting about 1,700 products: clothing, housewares, firearms, dry goods, jewelry, more. Invaluable for dating, identifying vintage items. Also, copyright-free graphics for artists, designers. Co-published with Henry Ford Museum & Greenfield Village. 160pp. 8¼ x 11. 25780-0 Pa. $10.95

HISTORIC COSTUME IN PICTURES, Braun & Schneider. Over 1,450 costumed figures in clearly detailed engravings–from dawn of civilization to end of 19th century. Captions. Many folk costumes. 256pp. 8⅜ x 11¾. 23150-X Pa. $12.95

STICKLEY CRAFTSMAN FURNITURE CATALOGS, Gustav Stickley and L. & J. G. Stickley. Beautiful, functional furniture in two authentic catalogs from 1910. 594 illustrations, including 277 photos, show settles, rockers, armchairs, reclining chairs, bookcases, desks, tables. 183pp. 6½ x 9¼. 23838-5 Pa. $11.95

AMERICAN LOCOMOTIVES IN HISTORIC PHOTOGRAPHS: 1858 to 1949, Ron Ziel (ed.). A rare collection of 126 meticulously detailed official photographs, called "builder portraits," of American locomotives that majestically chronicle the rise of steam locomotive power in America. Introduction. Detailed captions. xi + 129pp. 9 x 12. 27393-8 Pa. $13.95

AMERICA'S LIGHTHOUSES: An Illustrated History, Francis Ross Holland, Jr. Delightfully written, profusely illustrated fact-filled survey of over 200 American lighthouses since 1716. History, anecdotes, technological advances, more. 240pp. 8 x 10¾. 25576-X Pa. $12.95

TOWARDS A NEW ARCHITECTURE, Le Corbusier. Pioneering manifesto by founder of "International School." Technical and aesthetic theories, views of industry, economics, relation of form to function, "mass-production split" and much more. Profusely illustrated. 320pp. 6⅛ x 9¼. (USO) 25023-7 Pa. $9.95

HOW THE OTHER HALF LIVES, Jacob Riis. Famous journalistic record, exposing poverty and degradation of New York slums around 1900, by major social reformer. 100 striking and influential photographs. 233pp. 10 x 7⅞. 22012-5 Pa. $11.95

FRUIT KEY AND TWIG KEY TO TREES AND SHRUBS, William M. Harlow. One of the handiest and most widely used identification aids. Fruit key covers 120 deciduous and evergreen species; twig key 160 deciduous species. Easily used. Over 300 photographs. 126pp. 5⅜ x 8½. 20511-8 Pa. $3.95

COMMON BIRD SONGS, Dr. Donald J. Borror. Songs of 60 most common U.S. birds: robins, sparrows, cardinals, bluejays, finches, more–arranged in order of increasing complexity. Up to 9 variations of songs of each species. Cassette and manual 99911-4 $8.95

ORCHIDS AS HOUSE PLANTS, Rebecca Tyson Northen. Grow cattleyas and many other kinds of orchids–in a window, in a case, or under artificial light. 63 illustrations. 148pp. 5⅜ x 8½. 23261-1 Pa. $5.95

MONSTER MAZES, Dave Phillips. Masterful mazes at four levels of difficulty. Avoid deadly perils and evil creatures to find magical treasures. Solutions for all 32 exciting illustrated puzzles. 48pp. 8¼ x 11. 26005-4 Pa. $2.95

MOZART'S DON GIOVANNI (DOVER OPERA LIBRETTO SERIES), Wolfgang Amadeus Mozart. Introduced and translated by Ellen H. Bleiler. Standard Italian libretto, with complete English translation. Convenient and thoroughly portable–an ideal companion for reading along with a recording or the performance itself. Introduction. List of characters. Plot summary. 121pp. 5¼ x 8½. 24944-1 Pa. $3.95

TECHNICAL MANUAL AND DICTIONARY OF CLASSICAL BALLET, Gail Grant. Defines, explains, comments on steps, movements, poses and concepts. 15-page pictorial section. Basic book for student, viewer. 127pp. 5⅜ x 8½. 21843-0 Pa. $4.95

BRASS INSTRUMENTS: Their History and Development, Anthony Baines. Authoritative, updated survey of the evolution of trumpets, trombones, bugles, cornets, French horns, tubas and other brass wind instruments. Over 140 illustrations and 48 music examples. Corrected and updated by author. New preface. Bibliography. 320pp. $5\frac{3}{8}$ x $8\frac{1}{2}$. 27574-4 Pa. $9.95

HOLLYWOOD GLAMOR PORTRAITS, John Kobal (ed.). 145 photos from 1926-49. Harlow, Gable, Bogart, Bacall; 94 stars in all. Full background on photographers, technical aspects. 160pp. $8\frac{3}{8}$ x $11\frac{1}{4}$. 23352-9 Pa. $12.95

MAX AND MORITZ, Wilhelm Busch. Great humor classic in both German and English. Also 10 other works: "Cat and Mouse," "Plisch and Plumm," etc. 216pp. $5\frac{3}{8}$ x $8\frac{1}{2}$. 20181-3 Pa. $6.95

THE RAVEN AND OTHER FAVORITE POEMS, Edgar Allan Poe. Over 40 of the author's most memorable poems: "The Bells," "Ulalume," "Israfel," "To Helen," "The Conqueror Worm," "Eldorado," "Annabel Lee," many more. Alphabetic lists of titles and first lines. 64pp. $5\frac{3}{16}$ x $8\frac{1}{4}$. 26685-0 Pa. $1.00

PERSONAL MEMOIRS OF U. S. GRANT, Ulysses Simpson Grant. Intelligent, deeply moving firsthand account of Civil War campaigns, considered by many the finest military memoirs ever written. Includes letters, historic photographs, maps and more. 528pp. $6\frac{1}{8}$ x $9\frac{1}{4}$. 28587-1 Pa. $12.95

AMULETS AND SUPERSTITIONS, E. A. Wallis Budge. Comprehensive discourse on origin, powers of amulets in many ancient cultures: Arab, Persian Babylonian, Assyrian, Egyptian, Gnostic, Hebrew, Phoenician, Syriac, etc. Covers cross, swastika, crucifix, seals, rings, stones, etc. 584pp. $5\frac{3}{8}$ x $8\frac{1}{2}$. 23573-4 Pa. $15.95

RUSSIAN STORIES/PYCCKNE PACCKA3bl: A Dual-Language Book, edited by Gleb Struve. Twelve tales by such masters as Chekhov, Tolstoy, Dostoevsky, Pushkin, others. Excellent word-for-word English translations on facing pages, plus teaching and study aids, Russian/English vocabulary, biographical/critical introductions, more. 416pp. $5\frac{3}{8}$ x $8\frac{1}{2}$. 26244-8 Pa. $9.95

PHILADELPHIA THEN AND NOW: 60 Sites Photographed in the Past and Present, Kenneth Finkel and Susan Oyama. Rare photographs of City Hall, Logan Square, Independence Hall, Betsy Ross House, other landmarks juxtaposed with contemporary views. Captures changing face of historic city. Introduction. Captions. 128pp. $8\frac{1}{4}$ x 11. 25790-8 Pa. $9.95

AIA ARCHITECTURAL GUIDE TO NASSAU AND SUFFOLK COUNTIES, LONG ISLAND, The American Institute of Architects, Long Island Chapter, and the Society for the Preservation of Long Island Antiquities. Comprehensive, well-researched and generously illustrated volume brings to life over three centuries of Long Island's great architectural heritage. More than 240 photographs with authoritative, extensively detailed captions. 176pp. $8\frac{1}{4}$ x 11. 26946-9 Pa. $14.95

NORTH AMERICAN INDIAN LIFE: Customs and Traditions of 23 Tribes, Elsie Clews Parsons (ed.). 27 fictionalized essays by noted anthropologists examine religion, customs, government, additional facets of life among the Winnebago, Crow, Zuni, Eskimo, other tribes. 480pp. $6\frac{1}{8}$ x $9\frac{1}{4}$. 27377-6 Pa. $10.95

THE INFLUENCE OF SEA POWER UPON HISTORY, 1660–1783, A. T. Mahan. Influential classic of naval history and tactics still used as text in war colleges. First paperback edition. 4 maps. 24 battle plans. 640pp. 5⅜ x 8½. 25509-3 Pa. $14.95

THE STORY OF THE TITANIC AS TOLD BY ITS SURVIVORS, Jack Winocour (ed.). What it was really like. Panic, despair, shocking inefficiency, and a little heroism. More thrilling than any fictional account. 26 illustrations. 320pp. 5⅜ x 8½. 20610-6 Pa. $8.95

FAIRY AND FOLK TALES OF THE IRISH PEASANTRY, William Butler Yeats (ed.). Treasury of 64 tales from the twilight world of Celtic myth and legend: "The Soul Cages," "The Kildare Pooka," "King O'Toole and his Goose," many more. Introduction and Notes by W. B. Yeats. 352pp. 5⅜ x 8½. 26941-8 Pa. $8.95

BUDDHIST MAHAYANA TEXTS, E. B. Cowell and Others (eds.). Superb, accurate translations of basic documents in Mahayana Buddhism, highly important in history of religions. The Buddha-karita of Asvaghosha, Larger Sukhavativyuha, more. 448pp. 5⅜ x 8½. 25552-2 Pa. $12.95

ONE TWO THREE . . . INFINITY: Facts and Speculations of Science, George Gamow. Great physicist's fascinating, readable overview of contemporary science: number theory, relativity, fourth dimension, entropy, genes, atomic structure, much more. 128 illustrations. Index. 352pp. 5⅜ x 8½. 25664-2 Pa. $8.95

ENGINEERING IN HISTORY, Richard Shelton Kirby, et al. Broad, nontechnical survey of history's major technological advances: birth of Greek science, industrial revolution, electricity and applied science, 20th-century automation, much more. 181 illustrations. ". . . excellent . . ."–*Isis*. Bibliography. vii + 530pp. 5⅜ x 8¼. 26412-2 Pa. $14.95

DALÍ ON MODERN ART: The Cuckolds of Antiquated Modern Art, Salvador Dalí. Influential painter skewers modern art and its practitioners. Outrageous evaluations of Picasso, Cézanne, Turner, more. 15 renderings of paintings discussed. 44 calligraphic decorations by Dalí. 96pp. 5⅜ x 8½. (USO) 29220-7 Pa. $4.95

ANTIQUE PLAYING CARDS: A Pictorial History, Henry René D'Allemagne. Over 900 elaborate, decorative images from rare playing cards (14th–20th centuries): Bacchus, death, dancing dogs, hunting scenes, royal coats of arms, players cheating, much more. 96pp. 9¼ x 12¼. 29265-7 Pa. $12.95

MAKING FURNITURE MASTERPIECES: 30 Projects with Measured Drawings, Franklin H. Gottshall. Step-by-step instructions, illustrations for constructing handsome, useful pieces, among them a Sheraton desk, Chippendale chair, Spanish desk, Queen Anne table and a William and Mary dressing mirror. 224pp. 8⅛ x 11¼. 29338-6 Pa. $13.95

THE FOSSIL BOOK: A Record of Prehistoric Life, Patricia V. Rich et al. Profusely illustrated definitive guide covers everything from single-celled organisms and dinosaurs to birds and mammals and the interplay between climate and man. Over 1,500 illustrations. 760pp. 7½ x 10⅛. 29371-8 Pa. $29.95

Prices subject to change without notice.

Available at your book dealer or write for free catalog to Dept. GI, Dover Publications, Inc., 31 East 2nd St., Mineola, N.Y. 11501. Dover publishes more than 500 books each year on science, elementary and advanced mathematics, biology, music, art, literary history, social sciences and other areas.